P9-CDT-013

LAST CLIMB

CAPTIONS FOR GATEFOLDS

FIRST: *A jungle camp in Tibet during the 1922 British Mount Everest Expedition*

SECOND: *Expedition caravan crossing the windswept Tibetan plateau, spring 1922*

THIRD: *With Everest towering behind, the monastery at Rongbuk welcomed the 1922 expedition. Monks in the foreground are dwarfed by the monastery's chorten.*

Copyright information and CIP data can be found on page 239

THE LEGENDARY EVEREST EXPEDITIONS OF GEORGE MALLORY

LAST CLIMB

DAVID BREASHEARS
AND AUDREY SALKELD

FOREWORD BY JOHN MALLORY

NATIONAL GEOGRAPHIC
WASHINGTON, D. C.

CONTENTS

"DEAREST ONE, YOU MUST KNOW THAT THE SPUR TO DO MY BEST IS YOU AND YOU AGAIN," GEORGE MALLORY WROTE TO HIS BELOVED WIFE, RUTH. "I WANT MORE THAN ANYTHING TO PROVE WORTHY OF YOU."

IN MEMORIAM

The recent discovery of my father George Mallory's body high on Mount Everest has aroused new interest and speculation about the circumstances surrounding his disappearance on that fateful day 75 years ago. I had imagined that nightfall or foul weather had overtaken him and his climbing partner Andrew Irvine on their way down, possibly from the summit. Now it is clear to me that there was a fall, very likely after dark as Mallory's goggles were found in his pocket. Death followed fairly quickly.

I do not imagine that this or any book can shed new light on the events of that day. I do believe, however, that *Last Climb* will add considerably to our understanding of the sort of people these early pioneers were, and the extreme difficulties they faced. Members of the 1920s expeditions to Mount Everest had little knowledge of the mountain, and climbed with equipment that can only be described as primitive by today's standards.

I first traveled to Nepal in 1987 to enjoy the beauty and grandeur of the Himalaya, and trekked to within six miles of Mount Everest. The journey was a pilgrimage to honor a father I never really knew, for I was just three-and-a-half-years old when he left home for the last time. It was 1924, and in the first three years of my life, my father had journeyed twice to Everest, and to the United States for a lecture tour.

My most memorable Everest experience, however, took place in 1995, and David Breashears and Audrey Salkeld figured prominently in it. I first met them in 1986, and a few years later David suggested taking me to the North Ridge Base Camp, the site first chosen by my father in 1921. His idea was that together we would rebuild the stone memorial that had been erected by the surviving members of the 1924 expedition before they returned home, but which no longer existed.

I suggested that we go in 1995 as that year my wife Jenny and I were planning a trip to Nepal. We met in Kathmandu on April 26 and left for Tibet on May 1. Audrey and David had commissioned a beautiful memorial plaque made from Welsh slate to commemorate the British climbers of Mallory's era who had all climbed in Wales. The 66-pound plaque was carried by hand to Kathmandu, where we collected it, transporting it from there to Base Camp ourselves. Along the way, a landslide completely obliterated a treacherous section of the road, briefly halting our ascent to the Tibetan Plateau.

What an experience that journey was for me. Crossing a 17,200-foot pass called the Pang La, I had my first view of Mount Everest from the north side—the same view my father must have had so many years before. Strong, icy winds scoured the Pang La, making it an inhospitable place from which to admire the inspiring view. We later passed the Rongbuk Monastery before finally reaching base camp, with the great Mount Everest looming high in the sky only 12 miles away.

We were welcomed by Paul Pfau, the leader of an American

expedition that included our son, George, who would be making his own summit bid in the coming days. The next morning David and I chose a site for the new memorial on a small hillock above Base Camp, just a few feet away from the site of the previous one. We uncrated the plaque, and I was delighted by the beauty of its inscribed, dark gray slate. David quickly began work constructing the memorial with the help of a few Sherpas. That afternoon George returned to Base Camp for a few days of rest and good food before tackling the summit.

Shortly after sunrise two days later, before the cold wind started to blow, we dedicated the new plaque. It was such a poignant occasion that I briefly found myself unable to speak. I was wondering whether my father, as he gazed at Everest more than 70 years earlier, could have imagined that the three-year-old son he left behind would one day stand on the same spot to honor him.

I now realize it was a wistful thought, for George Mallory could not have foreseen the disaster that overtook him. What I finally did say on that bright clear morning was that I hoped the memorial would act as a reminder to future generations of mountaineers to have a sufficient reserve of time and energy for a safe descent. I do not believe that reaching the summit of a mountain, even Mount Everest, is worth losing one's life for.

Eight days later, on May 14, Jenny and I arrived home in South Africa, and were surprised with a phone call from Paul Pfau, who elatedly informed us that our son George had reached the summit of Mount Everest at 5:30 a.m. that morning. It was a wonderful moment. At long last a Mallory had stood atop Everest and had returned safely, completing the journey my father had begun in 1921, on the route he had pioneered.

I am proud of my son's achievement, and my father's. But I would so much rather have known my father than to have grown up in the shadow of a legend, a hero, as some people perceive him to be.

JOHN MALLORY *July 1999, Pretoria, South Africa*

HIGH WINDS SWIRL ABOVE MOUNT EVEREST, VIEWED HERE FROM THE SITE OF BASE CAMP FOR THE 1920S BRITISH EXPEDITIONS.

PROLOGUE

For the stone from the top for geologists,
the knowledge of the limits of endurance for the doctors,
but above all for the spirit of adventure
to keep alive the soul of man.

GEORGE MALLORY, 1923
ON WHY HE CLIMBED EVEREST

LOOKING FOR MALLORY

During the 1921 Everest reconnaissance George Mallory led a small party around to the east of Everest. West of Kharta, he entered the lush Kama Valley and climbed through forests of dwarf rhododendrons to camp at Pethang Ringmo, where he caught his first view of the massive, ice-hung Kangshung Face of Everest. This preposterous face, rising straight out of the glacier and soaring two miles into the sky, dashed his hopes of finding a route up the world's highest mountain from this side. Happy to leave the steep, snow-heavy facade for "other men, less wise," he concentrated his efforts elsewhere.

Sixty years later David Breashears was among the first team of "other men" sufficiently lacking in wisdom to take on this awesome challenge. With his friend Andrew Harvard, he stood where Mallory first stood, gazing at the great flying buttresses and hanging glaciers of the Kangshung Face and conceded that the old-world British mountaineer had a point.

Many times on that trip David found himself thinking about George Mallory, whose footsteps he and Harvard had followed. They had camped at his campsites, read his contributions in the book of that reconnaissance, rejoiced with him at visions of some of the finest mountain scenery in the world. Often it seemed George Mallory was there with them. It awakened in Breashears a lifelong fascination, not just with Mallory but with the whole company of Everest pioneers, who had launched themselves at a mountain no Westerner had seen at close quarters. With equipment and clothing we would consider grossly inadequate today, they ventured into atmospheres thinner than any earthbound travelers had experienced. For its day, going to Everest was like going to the moon.

My own Everest researches began a few years earlier, when I discovered the cornucopia of files at the Royal Geographical Society in London, inherited from the Mount Everest Committee. They contained almost every piece of paper written to or by that committee since its first overtures to the India Office in 1919, for permission to go to Tibet and attempt Everest, to the eventual ascent of the mountain by Col. John Hunt's party in 1953. Like David, I was hooked on this fascinating adventure story.

In 1985, David and I met through our mutual friend and fellow Everest historian, Tom Holzel. Tom wanted to search for Mallory and Irvine, and had obtained a precious permit to take an expedition to the Tibetan side of Everest the following year. Tom had been raising hackles in traditional mountaineering circles for over a decade with his maverick theories of what might have happened on that fateful climb. The accepted version was that the pair had died together before reaching their goal, but Tom held that Mallory, at least, could have reached the summit. His alternative scenario required the two men to have separated, giving Mallory his companion's oxygen supply and thus a better chance of success. He believed that if either man were carrying a camera, an exposed film may yet survive in the Everest snows. Processed with care, it could reveal a summit photograph. In the post-monsoon of that year, with Andy Harvard as leader, David as climbing leader, and Tom and I in the hitherto unknown roles of "Everest historians," we went to the north side of Everest.

It was a season of heavy winds and storms and the mountain lay under a mantle of deep snow. We failed to get high enough to look for Mallory and Irvine, finding only a few relics of the earlier expeditions around the lower campsites, but we did feel we knew Mallory a little better and certainly appreciated the phenomenal amount of ground he and Guy Bullock covered in their 1921 reconnaissance sorties.

As research for a film about the mystery, David and I, before and after our expedition, had crossed England and Wales in my blue Volkswagen Beetle, visiting Everesters, their wives, sons, and daughters and learning all we could about the pioneer adventurers. Our great good fortune was to come to this subject at a time when there were still climbers around from the 1920s and 1930s with firsthand stories to tell: There is nothing as thrilling as sitting in a room with someone who can build for you, with his memories, a living bridge to the past.

Noel Odell remembered sharing a tent with General Bruce just before bad health forced him to give up the leadership of the 1924 expedition. "He was wheezing and coughing and shaking like an earthquake," he said. "An enormous man. He had gone on a tiger hunt before the expedition. Bagged his tiger but picked up malaria."

A tall man, Odell was still erect in his 90s, and his long memory was intact. He had remarkable eyesight, too, driving his Morris Minor around town without spectacles; that in itself had significance, we felt. He was ponderous and methodical, a stickler for detail. The day we interviewed him in Cambridge, we had lunch first at the University Centre while the camera was set up in another room. The chef's special that day was baby goat. "Extraordinary!" Odell said. "The last time I had goat was in the Rongbuk Valley in Tibet." As the afternoon wore on, more memories were triggered.

We wondered why Mallory had chosen Irvine rather than Odell for that last climb. He'd spoken to Mallory about it, he said. "I told him frankly that my interest in the mountain was not only to climb it but also to know something of its geology." But he added, wistfully, "I would have been willing to forego my interest in the scientific side...and have gone with him...I shouldn't have minded reaching the top of Everest."

A year older than Odell was Capt. John Noel, whom we visited several times. One night early in 1986 before we went to Everest, Noel showed us in his darkened living room his Everest slides, giving us, in his old-fashioned diction essentially the same lecture that he told us proudly he had taken 14 times across America. At 96, the sonorous voice was a little tremulous, but he was a showman still. "What an adventure! These regions had never suffered the foot of man before we went there. The Tibetans told us that. I asked them through my interpreter, 'In all your history, have your people ever been up the glaciers of Everest?' 'No, no, never. They are the abode of our Gods, and they are sacred regions.' That was the adventure—to go here where you know that since the beginning of the world no human being had been before."

After a short pause for dramatic effect, he continued. "Then to see this great mountain! When I first set eyes on it I just sat on the ground and gasped. I said to myself, 'Good God, could anybody get up to the top of that thing?' But we never voiced such an opinion, never asked a question like that. We just shut our mouths; it was a task we had to do and we got on with it."

Shortly afterward we met George Mallory's son, John, in London and took him to the National Film Archive to see Captain Noel's Everest films of 1922 and 1924. The film archive's copies had been modified to be shown at modern film speeds. Even so, the images were shaky and thin. Yet there was one memorable sequence where the Everest team is seen leaving the governor's residence in Darjeeling. They come down the steps and turn in front of the camera, chatting animatedly. John Mallory knew by heart all the published still photographs of these early expeditions, but never before had he seen the images move. Now they were coming to life before him. The young, eager man at the heart of the group, with such obvious energy and verve, was the father he never knew. And John was seeing him as a man of almost half his own age. It was an emotional moment.

Between us, David and I have spent almost 40 years trying to get to know George Mallory, through his writings, the memories of his friends and family, and by prizing away the incrustations of myth. We looked for him in his achievements—on British rocks, in the Alps, and on Everest, and in his writings. In no field can he be dismissed lightly. He remains enigmatic, although part of his enduring appeal, I feel sure, is that he speaks across generations. We recognize an essential fairness and honesty in the man, along with his tenacity and spirit.

Little did we know when we began this book, which we intended as an accessible and enduring record of the inspirational early Everest attempts, that the body of George Mallory would be discovered high on the mountain 75 years after his disappearance. The discovery captured popular imagination and has provided us with a number of clues, without demolishing the mystery and romance of the story. I always thought that to find the bodies of Mallory and Irvine would change everything, that one would be bound to think of them differently afterwards. I can't say that has happened. I am still amazed at what they achieved, and this is our tribute to them and their companions.

Facing Mount Everest, John Mallory stands on the Pang La. Seventy-four years earlier, his father viewed Everest from this same spot during the 1921 British reconnaissance expedition. Prayer flags mark the Pang La as a holy spot for Tibetans.

SHROUDED IN MONSOON SNOWS MOUNT EVEREST RISES 9,000 FEET ABOVE THE RONGBUK GLACIER.

FRIEND AND MENTOR, GEOFFREY YOUNG NICKNAMED GEORGE MALLORY "GALAHAD" FOR HIS PURE, QUESTING SPIRIT. THIS PASTEL OF MALLORY WAS DRAWN CIRCA 1909.

CHAPTER ONE

As I looked out of my tent in the early morning, while all below was still wrapped in a steely grey, far away in the distance the first streaks of dawn would be just gilding the snowy summits of Mount Everest, poised high in heaven as the spotless pinnacle of the world.

COL. FRANCIS YOUNGHUSBAND
AT KAMPA DZONG, DURING HIS MISSION TO TIBET, 1903

THE SPOTLESS PINNACLE

When news broke in 1924 that the British climber George Mallory and his compatriot Andrew Irvine had been lost on Everest, the shock was felt more keenly for the fact that Mallory's was already a household name. Ordinary people around the world had taken the notion of trying to climb the highest peak to their imagination; letters flowed in to the Mount Everest Committee in London with ingenious suggestions for tackling the problem. Newspapers and journals made a splash of the photographs taken crossing Tibet to reach the great mountain, and lantern-slide lectures of the earlier attempts were given in cities around Britain and in Europe. Mallory took his Everest presentation to the United States and Canada during the first three months of 1922. He was the only man to have been involved in all three of the Everest efforts launched during that decade, and he had captured hearts with his charming manner and undisputed courage. His friend Col. E. F. Norton described him as the

"living soul" of what had become known as the Everest "offensive." Paying tribute at the time of his death, Norton said, "We always regarded him as an ideal mountaineer, light, limber, and active, gifted with tremendous pace up and down hill, and possessing all the balance and technical proficiency on rock, snow, and ice which only years of experience give." But more than that, "The fire within made him really great, for it caused his spirit constantly to dominate his body to such an extent that, much as I have climbed with him, I can hardly picture his ever succumbing to exhaustion."

Mallory was a few days short of his 38th birthday when he died, and Irvine, barely 22. When it came to picking teams for those early expeditions in the wake of the Great War of 1914-18, there had been a dearth of young mountaineers—so many in every walk of life were lost or disabled, and the climbing circle was no exception to this. The average age on those first sorties to Everest was around 40 years. Irvine was the first to be chosen from the post-war generation. Though lacking in climbing experience, he was picked for his youth and strength—"our attempt to get one superman," Mallory had written—and he was introduced in dispatches as the team's "experiment." Mallory, who had given many youngsters their first taste of climbing, took Irvine under his wing from the start. They had become friendly on the boat to India, when George had written home that he seemed "sensible and not highly strung...one to depend on for everything perhaps except conversation."

Mallory's own sense of adventure had manifested itself early. As a lively small boy growing

An intellectual as well as an adventurer, Mallory steeped himself in the classics at Cambridge—where he forsook climbing in the Alps in favor of earning his degree. During the long nights in camp on Everest, Mallory enjoyed discussing great authors and their works with whichever expedition member was so inclined.

up in rural England toward the end of Queen Victoria's reign, he'd found endless opportunities for deeds of daring. Trees, drainpipes, roofs were there to be climbed, brooks to be jumped across. Family lore suggests Mallory's life progressed from one escapade to another. At around age eight, while on a seaside holiday at St. Bees, he decided to remain on a particular rock while the tide came in. It was a rough day, and he was quickly marooned by choppy water, which seethed and sucked among the surrounding rocks. His alarmed grandmother, higher up the beach, could see that his perch would be quickly covered, and she shouted for help. A man in a boat was able to rescue him. Years later, after George was lost on Everest, this man came forward again to say how well he remembered the composed little lad who had shown no vestige of panic.

This adventurous spirit, which to some extent was shared by his siblings, the Mallory children inherited from their mother. Annie Beridge Jebb, daughter of a middle-aged Derbyshire clergyman and his younger, second wife, was born after her father had died of tuberculosis. She grew up fearless, fun-loving, and headstrong. In an endeavor to curb her high spirits, her mother insisted that she attend church twice on Sundays and go to Sunday school when she was old enough. As a result, Annie developed a strong, simple faith that never wavered. She was pretty and impulsive ("I always managed to lead boys and dogs into mischief," she would tell her grandchildren) and before she was 18 she was engaged to the kindly, mild-mannered Herbert Leigh Mallory. A student at the nearby theological college, Mallory was the 11th child of the vicar of Mobberley, and destined to follow in his father's footsteps. They married as soon as Herbert was ordained. In 1885, the year before George Mallory was born, Herbert took over the Mobberley church and congregation on the death of his father.

George was the second child and elder son of Herbert and Annie. He was an attractive child, singularly good looking, easy natured, and a hero to his two sisters, who vied for his attention. It was always so much fun doing anything with George, his younger sister Avie recalled; he had the knack for making things exciting and often rather dangerous, "I learnt very early that it was fatal to tell him that any tree was impossible for him to get up. 'Impossible' was a word that acted as a challenge to him.When he once told me that it would be quite easy to lie between the railway lines and let a train go over him, I kept very quiet, as if I thought it would be quite an ordinary thing to do; otherwise, I was afraid he would do it. He used to climb...about on the roof with cat-like sure-footedness."

George won a mathematical scholarship to Winchester College, where he was good at games and gymnastics. When his housemaster offered him the opportunity of a trip to the Alps during the school holidays in 1904, he

Mallory (at right) pioneered a new route on Lliwedd in North Wales over the 1913 Christmas holiday, posing afterward with climbing partner Siegfried Herford at Pen-y-Pass. Walking in the Welsh hills with friends Cottie Sanders and her brother Jack (opposite), George carried a long ice ax, a habit that would help prepare him for his Everest years. From his youngest days, George seemed determined to climb everything in sight, his sister Avie recalled.

begged his parents to let him go. This was during the summer when George was 18. He and a friend accompanied the teacher, Graham Irving, on what proved for Mallory a life-changing adventure. The following year Irving took Mallory to the Alps again, this time with new recruits added to the party. One, Guy Bullock, impressed everyone with his stamina and sound sense. "A tough sort of fellow who never lost his head and would stand any amount of knocking about," Mallory would later testify when candidates were being sought for Everest.

That year, soon after returning from Switzerland, Mallory went to Cambridge, and it would be several seasons before he returned to the Alps. He read history at Magdalene College, where his supervising tutor, Arthur Benson, encouraged his talent for writing and debate. A friend, David Pye, remembers Mallory at this time as very contentious, "a most persistent and even derisive arguer, who was apt to express himself disdainfully and contemptuously, and to shift his ground." Admitting that these were faults of youth, born of an enthusiasm that got the better of his sense of humor, Pye added that in conversation, too, Mallory was not always easy to follow. He tended to talk in rapid bursts, so that "many words got their wings clipped in the process." For all that, there was no hostility in his argumentativeness. Once the debate was over, differences were forgotten, and George returned to his usual warm self. He loved making friends, loved conversation, and would strike up acquaintances in train carriages, or anywhere, for the joy of discovering new people, new ideas, and new ways of looking at things.

While Mallory may not have been a seminal figure in the close Cambridge circle surrounding the poet Rupert Brooke, a clique dubbed by Virginia Woolf as "the Neo-Pagans," he and Brooke were near contemporaries and shared close friends in James and Lytton Strachey, Maynard and Geoffrey Keynes, the Pyes (David and his sisters), and Jacques Raverat, among many others. They each attended the soirees of the Cambridge underlibrarian, Charles Sayle, and through their common interests (the Fabian Society, literary matters, amateur dramatics) saw each other regularly throughout their overlapping years at university. Brooke remarked to one of his intimates in 1912 that he was "rather fond" of Mallory, but generally had "a vague feeling in his presence—as if I'm, momentarily, dull." When Rupert died on the Greek island of Skyros in 1915, George wrote, "It seems so wanton, and somehow it's a blow under the belt. He was a lovable person, and besides he had gifts. I never much believed that he had it in him to be a great poet, but after all he might have become one."

These early Edwardian years were a time of excitement and energy. At Cambridge the predominant mood was one of innovation and idealism, a conscious shaking off of Victorian thought and restraint; it was an age of artistic expression and free inquiry. The Neo-Pagans were dedicated to enjoyment and the cult of friendship; they espoused the "simple life," loved the outdoors, nude bathing, sleeping under the stars, but their hedonism was blurred with a developing social conscience. If Mallory was only peripherally involved in their reading parties and frolics—initially he seemed to prefer solemn discourse with older friends—he certainly shared their appetite for political exploration and reform. The university's branch of the Fabian Society was founded in 1906, and Mallory joined it—very much to his father's dismay. This was a time when Fabianism itself was going through a revolution under the influence of H. G. Wells and his "Constructive Socialism." Each individual in Wells' brave new world-order would "give whatever gifts he had as artist, as writer, as maker of any sort to increasing and refining the conception of civilized life." The philosophy appealed to Mallory, who was debating whether to follow his father into the church, but he remained unwilling to surrender free thought to religious orthodoxy. He began considering education as a profession.

In September 1907, with Geoffrey Keynes and Hugh Wilson, Mallory spent ten days in North Wales climbing and bathing in mountain streams. All three returned wondering if ever they would enjoy such bliss again. The following August George took his young brother, Trafford, climbing. By this time the family had moved from Mobberley to Birkenhead—a rather abrupt decision, taken it seems because Annie was developing an attachment for someone else in the village—and the two brothers set off from the Birkenhead vicarage on their bikes. Their mother received a letter from North Wales, where they were staying in a cow-shed beside the River Llugwy. Trafford (now 16) wrote: "There is the most glorious bathing among the rocks, there being one place in which one can sit and it

George's three expeditions to Tibet and his lecture tour in the United States kept him away from his wife Ruth and their three children, yet he professed undying devotion to his daughters, Clare (right) and Berridge, and son, John.

is as smooth and comfortable to sit in as a bath and the water comes up to the middle of one's chest. It is so absolutely glorious here that I cannot find words to express it, so George is going to have a turn at the pencil."

George continued: "Trafford really wants to have what he calls a bed rehearsal! And oh! What beds! Some feet of hay covered with blankets—no mattresses can beat that." They hoped that their sisters would be allowed to come and join them—"We intend to stay indefinitely," George wrote, "We can partition the hut." There were some home comforts lacking in their idyllic life, and George added: "When you send the shirts we would like a second tin mug which we can't procure here. The Welsh people are most kind and hospitable and we can get most things very easily. A home-made CAKE would be very pleasant."

The girls, hardly surprisingly for 1908, were not allowed to join their brothers. It was around this time that George is believed to have invented the Slab Climb on Lliwedd. Later in the year he and Geoffrey Keynes climbed in the Lake District, adding a few new routes to Gable Crag. In 1909, his final year at Cambridge, George was introduced to the climber Geoffrey Winthrop Young who would become a lifelong friend and mentor. Climbing assumed far greater importance to Mallory, not just as an active recreation, but in his consciousness.

Ten years older than Mallory, Young had a fine record of new Alpine routes, distinguished by their quality and aesthetic appeal; he was renowned for his long days in the mountains. A complicated character, precariously balancing the different compartments of his life, Young was a passionate friend and an inspirational teacher. He invited Mallory to join one of his legendary get-togethers at Pen-y-Pass in North Wales that Easter—so much talent, congeniality, and preposterous activity. A love of climbing was not the main requisite of invitees, nor indeed even necessary—for Young above all saw himself as a missionary, an advertisement for his beloved hills and for cultured, intergenerational fellowship. Evenings were for theatricals, singing, and competitive feats. Guests would include schoolmasters, dons, scientists, historians, old soldiers, athletes, undergraduates, young protégés, but—in the beginning at least—few women. After energetic days on the hills, they would relax in sitz baths around a blazing stove, shouting for the hotel staff to maintain the relays of hot water. "Unforgettable are the endless discussions of details of climbs from bath tub to bath tub," wrote Young, "...and George Mallory or young George Trevelyan leaping to do slow circles over the roof beam—until a blast of hail and protest let in the hot buckets and the boots together."

For two decades Young presided over his "hill company," which in time, as his own and his friends' family circumstances changed after World War I, did involve more women and even children. The climbs made during the hill company's early years account for much of the folklore of climbing, and Young's chivalrous ideals shaped the spirit of the sport, laying the foundations for so many of the ingrained ethics associated with mountaineering. Years later, Young would reflect with pride that it said "something perhaps for the calibre of the men first attracted by the romance of the hills, and of pioneer climbing, that of those who came on Pen-y-Pass parties, three earned the Order of Merit, four had the Nobel Prize, five became Cabinet ministers, seven were made peers and one a life peer, fifteen were knighted, and of course an indefinite number became honorary doctors."

Mallory passed his initiation into the group

This early portrait of Mount Everest was taken by J. Claude White during Col. Younghusband's 1903-4 mission to Tibet. Appearing as a ghost hovering above the horizon, Everest was, in Younghusband's words, "the spotless pinnacle of the world."

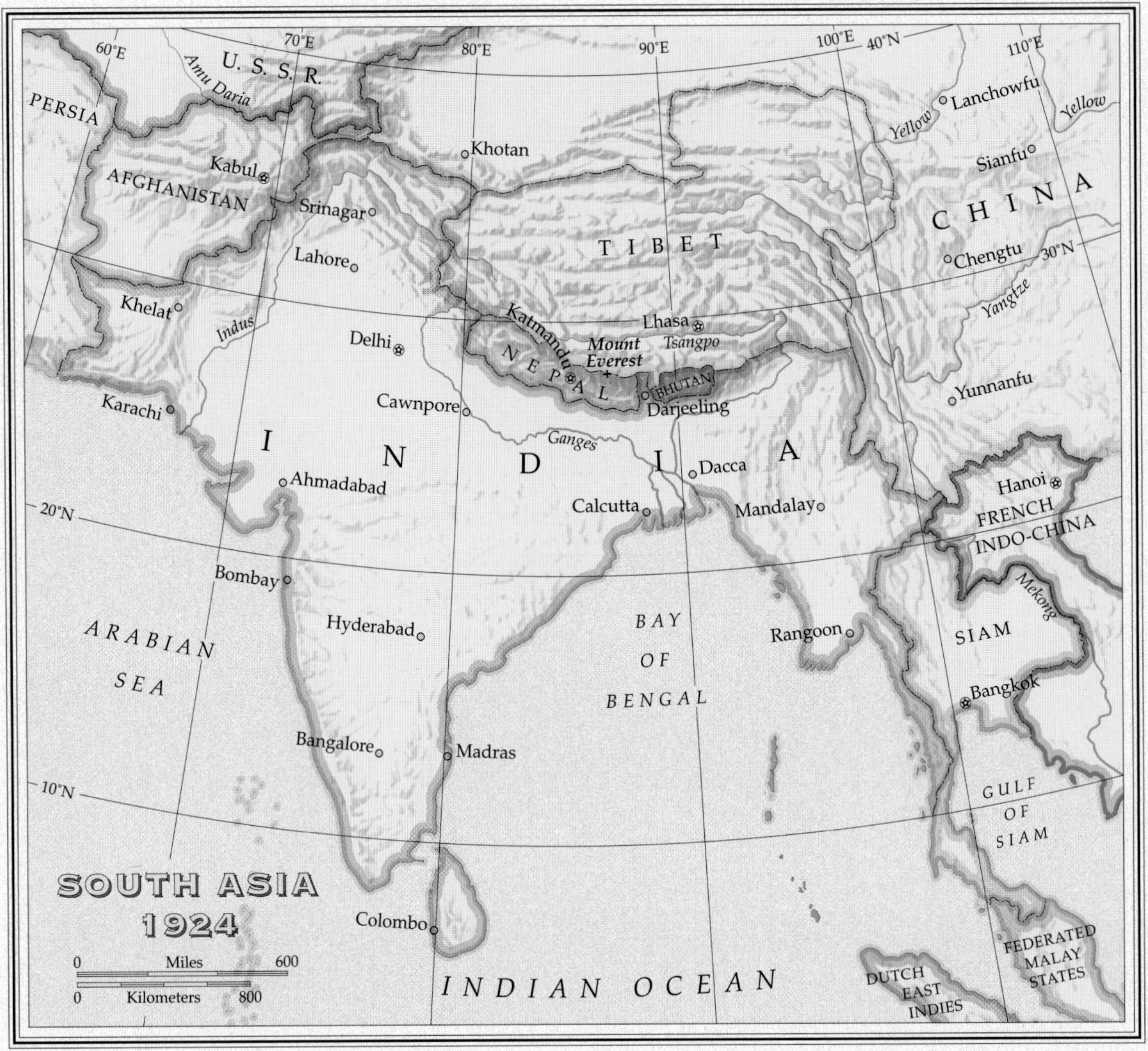

with flying colors, putting up a new route on Lliwedd with Edward Evans. Thinking they were repeating Great Chimney, they strayed onto slabs in the mist to produce what became known as Wrong Chimney. "He swung up rock with a long thigh, a lifted knee, and a ripple of irresistible movement," Young wrote of Mallory's climbing style. "A perfect physique and a pursuing mind came together as it were in a singleness of power, as he rushed into motion." In those days, when motor cars were rare and carts the most likely means of transport, getting to many of Snowdonia's remoter cliffs was difficult and slow, but the "mercurial Mallory might race over the ranges for the chance of finding a good crag, and return after nightfall. A Galahad (as he was called); chivalrous, indomitable, the splendid personification of youthful adventure; deer-like in grace and power of movement, self-reliant and yet self-effacing, and radiantly independent." Mallory frequently climbed the Welsh mountains alone, gaining a certain reputation for rashness that he considered ill-deserved, as did many of his close friends, who swore his strength and agility gave him an admirable technique with never a clumsy or ill-considered move.

In the summer of 1909, Mallory joined Young and Donald Robertson in the Alps, a season, Young wrote afterward, marked by "some hair-breadth happenings which are incidental to alpine inexperience." On one occasion Mallory forgot to tie in when leading off downhill and was startled on an insecure perch at the sound of Robertson, slipping off the rock behind him. Robertson's fall was stopped by the rope binding him and Young, who watched transfixed as Mallory spun round on his tiny "one-foot ice-nick" believing he would surely plunge to the glacier below. But the reassurance of a rope meant little to Mallory, who was "as sure-footed and as agile in recovery as the proverbial chamois." A day or two later, however, Mallory took a serious tumble, toward sunset, on the badly iced rocks of the virgin southeast ridge of the Nesthorn. He led out from a rock shelf at the foot of a dark tower that blocked the ridge, seeking a way upward. "So far as I could see," Young later wrote, "he had no real holds at all; but he fought his way up magnificently, until all that remained below the rock cornice, which cut off everything else above from my sight, were his two boots. These were clinging, cat-like, and continued to cling for long seconds, to almost imperceptible irregularities on the walls of the rift." Young instinctively tightened the rope, ready to "spring" should Mallory come unstuck. And then, when attempting a gymnastic swing up an overhang, Mallory came off. Young saw the boots flash from the wall and was aware of a soundless, gray streak flickering down past him, out of sight. "The clear fall could not have been much less than forty feet," he supposed. But the rope held, springing like an elastic band, as Young flung himself forward on to the belay, grinding it and his hands against the slab: "At first there was nothing to do but hold on, and watch the pendulum movement....My first cautious shouts were unanswered. Then, from nowhere, came a tranquil call to let out more rope, and to 'lower away.' Mallory was unhurt, unflustered, and had not even lost his ice ax."

Mallory left Cambridge with a lesser degree than he'd hoped, though Benson took much of the blame for this, saying he had encouraged reading and essay writing at the expense of strict adherence to the curriculum. After a few temporary posts and a period in the south of France perfecting his French, Mallory accepted a position as assistant master at Charterhouse School in Godalming in the Surrey countryside.

Mallory became a schoolmaster by conviction. Though at odds with much of the public school ethic, he firmly believed in the civilizing force of education and hoped that, by encouraging the young to think for themselves, lessons could be learned from history. World affairs, contemporary thinking, art, poetry, and literature were all introduced into his

VIEW FROM DARJEELING OF DEODHUNGA, THE HIGHEST MOUNTAIN IN THE WORLD, LATELY MEASURED BY
DRAWN BY S. READ, FROM A SKETCH BY CAPTAIN W. S. SHERWILL.—(SEE N

S. WAUGH, HEIGHT ABOVE THE SEA, 29,002 FEET.

everyday teachings and extramural activities. As weekends and holidays allowed, he traveled far to keep up with his widening circle of friends, planning complicated journeys to visit as many as possible, and to see all the latest art exhibitions. His friends, too, were always welcome to visit him at the school. He joined the Alpine Club. This period marked the time of his greatest involvement with the literary and artistic Bloomsbury set, the painter Duncan Grant becoming a special friend.

The Surrey countryside delighted him with its greenness. To a climbing friend, Cottie Sanders, he wrote: "Lord, it is good about here, particularly as I spend many glorious nights under the stars." That summer (1911) he went to the Alps with old friends Graham Irving and Harry Tyndale, where the culminating event was an ascent of Mont Blanc from the Col du Géant, traversing Mont Maudit. This memorable climb, probably a third ascent, occasioned one of his best essays for *The Alpine Journal*. Wryly, he told Geoffrey Young in a letter that the essay was being passed from one Alpine Club member to the next with no one knowing what to make of it. "I fear it's a wild performance—an attempt to treat an expedition as a spiritual experience with a great deal about states of mind and very little about the physical details." It concludes (on the dome of Mont Blanc): "Have we vanquished an enemy? None but ourselves. Have we gained success? That word means nothing here. Have we won a kingdom? No...and yes. We have achieved an ultimate satisfaction...fulfilled a

In 1857 the world's highest peak was yet to be named Everest.

destiny....To struggle and to understand—never this last without the other; such is the law...."

George had settled happily enough at Charterhouse, though friends later remarked that his talents were to an extent wasted there. Godalming proved an oasis of culture that suited him. Early in 1914, when taking part in an amateur dramatic production, George Mallory met the Turner sisters, who lived across the river from the school, at Westbrook, a fine house on a hill to the west of town. Marjorie, Ruth, and Mildred were the daughters of Thackeray Turner, an architect, once colleague and friend to the great designer-craftsman and social reformer William Morris. Their mother, Mary Turner, had died seven years earlier. Mr. Turner had built Westbrook himself in the style of Lutyens, a large, airy house with a lot of light wood paneling. Deep windowsills bore large china bowls, which he had hand-painted in formal Art Nouveau floral designs—kingcups, irises, peonies, water lilies. Mallory was soon a regular visitor at the house, if ostensibly to see the girls, as much to talk to or to play billiards with the old man. He had taken to giving regular art lectures at school and was thrilled to be hearing firsthand about the arts and crafts movement as he was about learning of the post-impressionists through Duncan Grant.

That Easter, Mallory was invited to join the Turners for a week in Venice. He leapt at the opportunity, which fitted in ideally with earlier plans to meet George Trevelyan and Will Arnold Foster for a week's walking in the Appenines. Italy was a delight, and on one day in flower meadows above Asolo, George and Ruth, the middle Turner daughter, declared their love for one another. "I had a glorious time in Venice," he wrote to his sister Avie, "and I left it with much regret." The week of walking gave him plenty of time to ruminate on the "furious revolution" he was undergoing. Within a week of his getting home, George and Ruth were engaged, and the wedding was planned for July. He wrote ecstatically to his mother, "She's as good as gold, and brave and true and sweet. What more can I say!"

Although its peak was visible from Darjeeling by telescope, Everest—tucked between its neighbor mountains Lhotse, left, and Makalu, right—hid its bulk from view. The only way to find a route to the top was to get beyond the barrier mountains and view Everest close-up.

Ruth Turner had what George would call "Botticellian" beauty, a rounded, tranquil face, with enormous china-blue eyes, framed with light hair worn in simple pre-Raphaelite style with an encircling braid. She was completely lacking in artifice and guile. George could not wait for Young to meet his fiancée. "Do come," he urged. And Young came at once—to be impressed. He had never met anyone, he said, who brought such an atmosphere of reality. "It is *big*, just *big*, that nature." Happy for his friend, he told him, "I could *shout*."

George's father performed the wedding ceremony, Geoffrey Young was best man. Guests were agreed that the happy couple looked too good to be true, but the proposed honeymoon in the Alps had to be canceled. War had broken out in Europe, and instead, the bridal pair went walking in Devon and

Sussex, where they camped on the beach one night—and were arrested briefly on suspicion of being German spies.

As a schoolmaster, George's was a reserved occupation, and he was not called up to fight. For a while in 1915, settling in to a new house, the Holt, and with Ruth expecting their first child, he was happy and content, but guiltily so. As time passed he became increasingly restless, particularly as friends and former students began dying at the front. He wanted to get into uniform and didn't really care whether it was the Flying Corps, the Royal Naval Air Service, or a desk job at the Admiralty, but his head-master refused to sanction his leaving. Early in 1916, a replacement was found for him at the school, and he was released to begin training as a second lieutenant in the Royal Garrison Artillery. He crossed to France on May 4.

Suddenly it all became real, even though his first posting was in a "quiet" place, with a good deal of protection. Separation from Ruth brought pangs. "Do let me hear that you are somehow happy, my poor dear Ruth," he wrote on his first night abroad. "I expect our faces will fly together in the night and kiss midway between France and England."

George enjoyed the campaigning side of army life. He would describe his dugout and made it sound quite homely with his cartridge box table, boards for a floor, string for clothes-line. The shiny black roof dripped, but he had

THE 1922 AND 1924 EVEREST EXPEDITIONS FOLLOWED A NEAR IDENTICAL

APPROACH ROUTE ESTABLISHED BY THE 1921 RECONNAISSANCE TRIP.

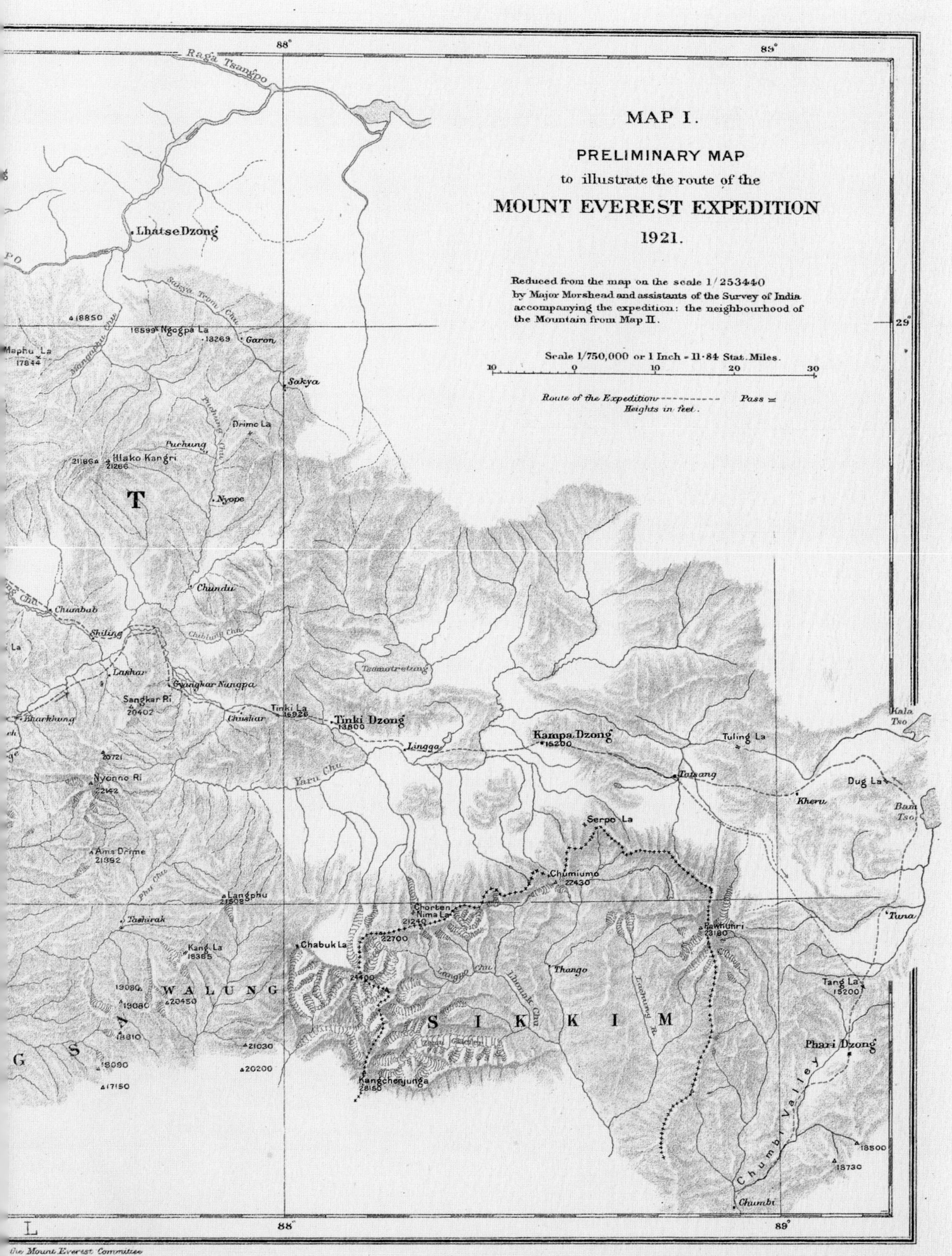

a suitcase for his treasures except, he told her, the little book with *Romeo and Juliet*, *Lear*, *Hamlet*, and *Othello*, which he generally kept in his pocket. Every three days a bath would be put out in the meadow behind. "No, I'm not bored and don't intend to be," and even if wet clay did get him down, the whole general way of life was somehow "youth-giving." Ruth's family teased her when they heard this: "Father said if you were going to get any younger he didn't know what would happen and Marjorie that I should be dandling you on the other arm with Clare. They are sillies."

Of course there were harsher realities and times when George and his comrades came under heavy fire. He was relieved to find that he did not faint or fade away at the sight of bodies, could keep his nerve and composure, and do what he should. "But oh! The pity of it!" he wrote, "and anger I feel too sometimes when I see corpses quite inexcusably not buried." In August he confessed that he'd had a narrow escape that he hadn't wanted to tell Ruth about at first. "But we settled long ago that there's no reckoning with Death. Everyone out here who goes anywhere near the fighting line has narrow escapes and you may have a million or a dozen. It worries me sometimes for you, dear one."

George was allowed a few days leave that Christmas, which if too short was, he told Ruth "more than all that I ever dreamed," but it was disconcerting on his return to find he had new duties. "I'm told I have to look after the Colonel, but damn it all, I'm not a valet. I have an admirable manner in passing the salt and offering whisky—in short it's a 'cushy' job, very quiet and safe in a little chalk gulley not far from the batteries." At the end of January he was offered the chance of applying for a job on staff, but as he told Ruth, "I don't think I could wear red hats....Somehow they don't seem to belong to the world of war except the bigpots." Soon afterward it was decided that George should be sent home to have an operation on an old ankle injury that had been giving him increasing trouble. He had broken it in a climbing fall in 1909 and had not sought treatment for it. This time it mended satisfactorily, and in August he was able to test it out on a short holiday in Scotland before reporting to an army camp near Winchester to await a posting. He was able to see Ruth on the weekends, as she drew closer to the birth of their second child, Berridge, who arrived at the start of the third week in September.

It was at this time news came that Geoffrey Young had been badly wounded in the battle for Monte San Gabriele, requiring his left leg to be amputated above the knee. George was appalled. "It's the spoiling of some flawless, perfect thing," he commisserated with Geoffrey's mother. "We had promised each other days on the mountains together—if we should meet again—and I can't separate my own loss in it from his."

George did not get back to France until the second half of September for the final months of the war. There was little to do and time to think and write. He turned his mind once more to his ideas for educational reform and to the *Book of Geoffrey*, a novel about a father and a son he had begun in 1915. And he dreamed of all the climbing trips he would make when things were back to normal.

For most of man's history no one knew what was the highest spot on Earth. And then, during the course of surveying and mapping India and the Himalaya, as successive peaks were plotted and measured in the 19th century, curiosity began to grow over which might prove the highest. There is a popular story telling how one day in 1852, the Bengali chief computer of the Survey of India rushed into the office of his superior, Sir Andrew Waugh, shouting, "Sir! Sir! I've discovered the highest mountain in the world!"

It is certain that after lengthy analysis of a series of triangulations, Waugh felt confident enough in March 1856 to announce what the Survey had long suspected: that the mountain identified by its Survey number Peak XV was "most probably the highest in the world." By collating measurements from various locations, an "unweighted average" of 29,002 feet had been obtained, which confirmed that Peak XV surpassed its nearest altitudinal rival, K2 in the Karakoram, which was assessed at 28,156 feet.

A mountain of such importance clearly needed a name, rather than a number, and within a few months Waugh was proposing it be called after his eminent predecessor at the Survey of India, the man who had instigated most of the great work of establishing the Great Arc of the Meridian, Sir George Everest. There is some irony to this, and even Sir George was not in agreement, since normal Survey policy was to establish the local names for geographical places, rather than to invent alien ones. Though it is now clear that Chomolungma, "Goddess Mother of the Land," was the Tibetan name by which the mountain was most widely known—Everest has remained in common use.

Once recognized as the world's pinnacle, it was natural for people to wonder if man (or woman) would ever tread Everest's summit. It is known that the American alpinist Miss Meta Brevoort was assembling information about the mountain during the summer of 1876. "No fear of wild beasts," she noted with satisfaction, "no rains at the proper season, nor hostile natives if one could get properly accredited," but what, she wondered, of the altitude? That was the problem. 29,002 feet were hard to envisage. An engineer on leave from India, helpfully pointed out to her by means of a cloud on the horizon, just how high that might look from a distance. She was undaunted. The attempt to climb Everest, however, was not to be: Death caught Miss Brevoort unawares later that year at the age of 50. Nevertheless, she had foreseen the advantage, if not necessity, of acquiring for such a venture the support of the Royal Geographical Society in London, the preeminent body concerned with exploration and science.

By the 1890s there was serious discussion among mountaineers and travelers about the problems Everest might pose. Capt. Charlie Bruce (as he then was) was one of the first to propose a reconnaissance of the mountain's approaches with a view to launching a determined bid on the summit. He and the soldier-traveler Francis Younghusband plotted and

In the forests of Tibet, expedition members raise their canvas tents among the trees and shrubs.

LUSH VEGETATION WAS A WELCOME CONTRAST TO THE BARREN TIBETAN PLATEAU.

planned with growing enthusiasm, but neither was in a position to bring their dreams to fruition at that time. In 1905 the matter was raised again when it was learned that Lord Curzon, then-Viceroy of India, was in favor of an attempt and would be prepared to contribute 3,000 pounds toward an expedition. This, too, came to nothing, through the veto of John Morley, secretary of state for India, who considered relations with India's neighbors, Tibet and Nepal, too fragile to risk a request for passage through either territory in order to reach the mountain.

Capt. John Noel did not ask for permission when he tried to see if he could reach Everest. In 1913, on leave from his Indian regiment, he slipped illicitly into Tibet over an unguarded pass with a small group of hill men. Then, taking a high-level route to avoid detection on the major trade thoroughfare, he bypassed the settlement of Kampa Dzong and was able to get within 40 or 50 miles of Everest before being turned back by armed guards. This foray was undertaken as a reconnaissance for a proposed expedition the following year to be led by Col. Rawling, which had the backing of the Royal Geographical Society and the Alpine Club. War intervened to interrupt these plans, and Rawling was one of many who did not survive to see the Armistice.

Outwardly, there was little change in attitude toward Tibet after the war. The secretary of state for India remained reluctant to cooperate as relations with Tibet were strained. There were also fears of "Japanese infiltration in that direction." Dr. T. G. Longstaff has written of the

The leader of the 1922 expedition, Gen. Charles Bruce, cools off at Rongpo Chu, a stream that also served as the team's swimming hole.

"hopeless frustration" of battling against political difficulties of access, saying, "it was only such difficulties which so long debarred us from exploring and attempting to climb Mount Everest." Yet, the urge to challenge these difficulties was gaining in strength. In 1919, when Sir Francis Younghusband was appointed president of the Royal Geographical Society (or the "Jog" as he liked to call it), he vowed that advances toward Everest, as the last major unsolved problem for geographers and mountaineers, would be made during his three years in office.

On March 10 Captain Noel gave an account to the Society of his attempt to reach Mount Everest from the northeast six years before. The discussion that followed left no doubt of popular support for Younghusband's latest mission. Dr. Alexander Kellas revealed that he had been considering the problem for many years and was collecting photographs of the objective from as many different directions as possible. He had two pictures showing the "North-East Glacier of Mount Everest," taken from a distance of 25 miles by one of his native assistants. The president of the Alpine Club registered full support for further exploration: The Club would lend such financial aid as was in its power, he said, and he could recommend two young mountaineers capable of dealing with any mountaineering difficulties to be met on Mount Everest. Colleagues knew him to be referring to George Mallory and George Ingle Finch.

GEORGE H. LEIGH MALLORY

ANDREW C. IRVINE

EVEREST TEAM MEMBERS

1921

Lt. Col. Charles K. Howard-Bury *(Leader)*

Harold Raeburn
(Climbing Leader, but indisposed)

George H. Leigh Mallory
(Acting Climbing Leader)

Guy H. Bullock

Dr. Alexander M. Kellas

Dr. A. M. Heron
(Geological Survey of India)

Maj. Henry T. Morshead
Maj. Edward O. Wheeler
(Survey of India)

Dr. Alexander F. R. Wollaston
(Medical Officer/Naturalist)

Gyalzen Kazi
Chettan Wangdi
(Interpreters)

1922

Brig. Gen. Charles G. Bruce
(Leader)

Lt. Col. Edward Lisle Strutt
(Deputy Leader)

Capt. C. Geoffrey Bruce
Colin G. Crawford
C. John Morris
(Transport Officers)

George Ingle Finch

Dr. Tom G. Longstaff
(Medical Officer/Naturalist)

George H. Leigh Mallory

Maj. Henry T. Morshead

Maj. Edward F. Norton

Capt. John B. L. Noel
(Photographer/Filmmaker)

Dr. T. Howard Somervell

Dr. Arthur W. Wakefield

Karma Paul
(Interpreter)

Gyaljen (Gyalzen Kazi)
(Sirdar)

1924

Brig. Gen. Charles G. Bruce
(Leader, but indisposed)

Lt. Col. Edward F. Norton
(Acting Leader, after Bruce taken ill)

George H. Leigh Mallory
(Climbing Leader)

Bentley Beetham

Capt. C. Geoffrey Bruce

John de Vars Hazard

Maj. R.W.G. Hingston
(Medical Officer)

Andrew C. Irvine

Capt. John B. L. Noel
(Photographer/Filmmaker)

Noel E. Odell

E. O. Shebbeare
(Transport Officer)

Dr. T. Howard Somervell

Karma Paul
(Interpreter)

Gyaljen (Gyalzen Kazi)
(Sirdar)

JELEP LA, THE GATEWAY TO THE TIBETAN PLATEAU, IS DEPICTED IN THIS 1922 WATERCOLOR BY COL. E.F. NORTON, PAINTED DURING THE EXPEDITION'S APPROACH MARCH.

CHAPTER TWO

As the clouds rolled asunder before the heights, gradually, very gradually, we saw the great mountainsides and glaciers and ridges, now one fragment, now another, through the floating rifts, until, far higher in the sky than imagination dared to suggest, a prodigious white fang—an excrescence from the jaw of the world— the summit of Everest, appeared.

GEORGE MALLORY LEAVING GYANGKAR NANGPA, 1921

WALKING OFF THE MAP

They were told it was too early in the season to take the short road between Phari and Kampa Dzong. The expedition was forced to adopt a roundabout route that kept them at high altitude and took twice as long. The final stretch involved crossing a 17,000-foot pass before descending through deep limestone gorges into Kampa. Men were still straggling into the walled enclosure that was to be their camp under the magnificent hill fort when a messenger ran up with alarming news. Dr. Kellas had died of heart failure crossing the last high pass. Their medical officer, Sandy Wollaston, jumped on his pony and returned up the valley to bring him in.

George Mallory was appalled. Kellas was the most experienced Himalayan traveler of them all, and the only man to have given serious thought not only to possible routes up Everest, but also to the whole science of acclimatization. He had been ill for over a week with what was thought to be enteritis, but had put such a brave face on his suffering

Mules and porters trudge along a worn path on the Tibetan Plateau, carrying food, tents, and climbing equipment. This panoramic photograph from the 1922 expedition illustrates the barren terrain traversed by the reconnaissance team in 1921.

that none suspected the seriousness of his condition. At Phari, there was talk of leaving him behind to recover, but it was such a bleak, unwholesome place—"the most incredibly dirty warren that can be imagined," in Mallory's view—that they had not insisted upon it, and Kellas himself wavered until it was too late. His porters rigged a chair to carry him, as he was not strong enough to walk or ride. When, at the last moment, his courage failed and he announced that it would be wiser for him to stay, it was too late. "All the troop, the cooks with their cooking pots, and everyone's kit, were spread across the plain," as Mallory confided in a letter. "To change plan was so difficult that Kellas was persuaded to come on."

There would be nowhere to stop before Kampa, but if the doctor was showing no improvement by then, a route existed from there by which he could be evacuated into Sikkim. "Generally speaking, after seeing him off, no one of us accompanied him," Mallory wrote, "and he arrived in camp two hours or so after the rest of us." In retrospect, this looked dangerously like neglect on their part, and Mallory's remorse was clearly evident: "Can you imagine anything less like a mountaineering party? He died without one of us anywhere near him. And yet it was a difficult position. The old gentleman (such he seemed) was

obliged to retire a number of times en route and could not bear to be seen in this distress, and so insisted that everyone should be in front of him. Well, once one is in front, one doesn't linger much in dusty places on the windswept plain; and after our first anxieties none of us lingered much for Kellas. After all, there was nothing to be done for him if one did stay...."

The death of Kellas was a disaster. Not only for the loss of a fine if unconventional man whom Mallory had eagerly looked forward to knowing better, but also for his unique experience. Kellas was the world's expert on mountain sickness and on the lassitude that was known to affect performance at high altitudes. For seven summers he had traveled and climbed in Kashmir, Sikkim, and the Garhwal Himalaya and was generally acknowledged to have been the first to recognize the superiority of Sherpas for rugged exploration work. Three of the great Sikkimese peaks, visible on the skyline from Kampa Dzong, had been first climbed by him: Chumiomo, Pawhunri, Kangchenjhau. He had undertaken experiments in pressure chambers with the celebrated scientist Professor Haldane, and had begun tests with bottled oxygen as an aid to climbing, work he had hoped to continue on this expedition.

A breakdown in his health in 1919 caused Kellas to resign his job as lecturer in chemistry at a London medical school, but within months he set off for the Himalaya, where he had been ever since. In December 1920, he followed the watershed between Sikkim and Nepal to reach the Kang La pass, near Kangchenjunga, to secure a shot of Mount Everest from 80 miles away. His telephotograph, published in *The Times* on March 18, 1921, captured the high mountains to the north of Everest that had never been surveyed or photographed.

When selected to go on the Everest reconnaissance, Kellas immediately began training a band of Sherpas to accompany him. While the team was assembling in Darjeeling, he was attempting to scale Kabru—with the intention of obtaining more photographs to help identify a possible climbing route on Everest. He arrived back at Darjeeling, late for "a swagger dinner party" given in honor of the team by His Excellency, Lord Ronaldshay, the Governor of Bengal. Mallory delightedly described to his wife Ruth the surreal contrast between the pomp of the occasion in Government House and the abrupt and distinctly unceremonious appearance of Kellas:

"It was a wonderful show. His Excellency entered and amid complete silence made the circuit of the room and shook hands with everyone. In the dining room a small host of native servants wearing long red coats ornamented with gold and silver braid pushed our chairs in as we sat down and poured champagne into our glasses after every sip.

"Kellas I love already. He is beyond description Scotch and uncouth in his speech. He arrived at the great dinner party ten

A view of eternity stretches below the stone marking the grave of Dr. A. M. Kellas, who died en route to Everest in 1921. A veteran of seven Himalayan expeditions, Kellas was laid to rest by the team at a spot that overlooked a series of peaks he had climbed on previous trips. Mallory wrote to his wife, "It has been a distressing business."

minutes after we sat down, and very disheveled, having walked in from Grom, a little place four miles away. His appearance would form an admirable model to the stage for a farcical representation of an alchemist. He is very slight in build, short, thin, stooping, and narrow-chested; his head a very curious shape, and made grotesque by veritable gig-lamps of spectacles and a long, pointed mustache. He is an absolutely devoted and disinterested person."

And now he was dead. Kellas had worn himself out before they started. No one expected that. Mallory, casting a jaundiced eye around his companions, reckoned their chances for success slim. He almost regretted coming. This was not an "easy party," as he confided to Ruth.

Mallory had needed little persuasion when the opportunity to go to Everest presented itself. Since coming home from the war he'd felt restless and unfulfilled. Like so many returning soldiers before and since, Mallory found it difficult to slip back into an unadventurous routine. His sense of anticlimax was compounded by an urge to improve the prevailing social and political climate. Teaching no longer offered the scope his idealism desired. If his role in life was to influence minds, then he wanted those minds to be more capable of response. He would prefer working with adults than young boys. In a letter addressed to Sir Gilbert Murray and dated June 1920, Mallory offered his services to the Union of the League of Nations, stressing how he thinks and feels "passionately" about international politics. It is not clear whether this offer was taken up, but later that year he went to Ireland to collect firsthand information of life there under the "Terror."

Mallory knew that exploring unknown Tibet and making a determined effort to climb the highest pinnacle on Earth would have no radical effect in reforming society, but the expedition would doubtless be inspirational, and could bring him celebrity and add a certain authority to his views. Besides, the enterprise would doubtless prove great fun. Any reservations that it might be regarded as a stunt were fleeting, quashed with the aid of Ruth's support and enthusiasm. Urging him to go, she told him that this could be the opportunity of a lifetime. When a formal invitation to join the reconnaissance party was put to him in February 1921, he accepted with alacrity, and at once resigned his mastership at Charterhouse. "The future bears rather an adventurous aspect altogether," he wrote to his sister Avie. "I shall be starting for Tibet early in April and have no very definite idea what I shall do after I come back in the autumn—except that there's much in my head which is asking to be written."

His elation suffered its first dent when he learned the proposed makeup of the party. Apart from himself and Finch, a strong alpinist two years his junior for whom he had the greatest respect (if not much affection), they appeared rather elderly or not to be real climbers. The leader, Col. Charles Kenneth Howard-Bury, had not been the Everest Committee's first choice. It wanted Gen. Charlie Bruce, a great mountain traveler and climber, who got on famously with Himalayan hill people, but the British Army could not

In the fortress town of Kampa Dzong, along the expedition trail in the Tibetan hills, Mallory photographed the fortified main building. He also took pictures of Bhotias at Linga (right). Born and raised at elevations above 10,000 feet, they were as nearly suited for the exhausting task of portering as anyone could be.

Dwarfed by Shegar Dzong, the "White Crystal Fort" as translated by the British, the 1922 expedition tents lie at the edge of the fortress town, exactly where they'd been erected in 1921. The monastery at Shegar Dzong clung to the sheer rock and was only reached by monstrous staircases.

spare him in 1921. And since this first effort was expected to be one of reconnaissance, it was deemed more important to secure Bruce's services for the climbing attempt that would most likely take place the following year. At his own expense, Howard-Bury had been to India and Tibet and had been instrumental in gaining permission from the Dalai Lama, for British climbers to go to Everest—a real coup after the years of fruitless applications through the India Office. Deeply in his debt, the committee offered him the leadership for 1921. His charge was to find a practicable route to the mountain, through country where the white men's maps ran out. If the opportunity to mount a climbing attempt was to emerge, as Mallory and

others hoped it would, that would be a bonus.

At 40, Howard-Bury was five years older than Mallory. His father died when he was just two, and he was placed under the guardianship of his cousin, then Viceroy of India. As a soldier and a young man of means, he seized every opportunity to travel, undertaking a six-month journey in the remote Tian Shan mountains. He was a natural linguist, fine photographer, keen plant collector, and a marksman. A man of strict order and discipline, he could be intimidating. Even at their first meeting in London, Mallory had found him difficult to like, and he never got over a sense of unease in his presence. "Not a tolerant person," he wrote to Ruth. "He is well-informed and opinionated and doesn't at all like anyone else to know things he doesn't know. For the sake of peace, I am being careful not to broach certain subjects of conversation."

Harold Raeburn, who was appointed "leader of the Alpine party," had been a

The interpreters for the 1921 expedition, Gyalzen Kazi and Chettan Wangdi, were enlisted by the team at Darjeeling.

guideless climber of great dash in his day, but his day was past. This tough, abstemious Scot infuriated Mallory and Finch when it came to ordering mountaineering equipment by wanting to cut down on items they considered vital, particularly with regard to provision for the inevitable cold they would encounter at great heights. He was touchy about taking advice, wanting to be treated with proper respect. Once on the road, Mallory made efforts to engage him and found him possessed of "a good deal of fatherliness and kindliness," although "his total lack of calm and a sense of humour at the same time is unfortunate."

From the outset this had seemed to Mallory an inadequate party. He couldn't foresee Raeburn or Kellas getting higher than 24,000 to 25,000 feet—any serious climbing attempt would therefore depend on him and Finch, unless one of the two surveyors attached to the expedition by the Survey of India took to climbing and made a success of it. To Geoffrey Young, Mallory had written, "Perhaps, after all, I shall be the weakest of the lot; but at present I feel more doubtful of Finch's health."

So, too, did the doctors, who were vetting the members of the expedition. A few weeks before they were due to leave, George Ingle Finch, perhaps the best alpinist of the day, was turned down on what seemed spurious medical grounds. The selection committee cast around for a replacement, but lacked inspiration. The Alpine Club's representative, Percy Farrar, would have been happy to extend the team to include talented foreign mountaineers, but others wanted it to remain "BAT"—as Bruce described it—"British All Through." When it looked as if another veteran would be added to their number, an exasperated Mallory pleaded the cause of a climbing friend he'd known since school days, Guy Bullock, who had just completed a diplomatic posting overseas and could be available at short notice. Bullock was promptly welcomed onto the team.

The climbing party of nine was completed with Kellas, the Survey of India men—Henry Morshead and Oliver Wheeler—a geologist A. M. Heron, and the explorer Sandy Wollaston, who would double up as medical officer and naturalist. They converged on the Himalaya from different directions, and Mallory found himself sailing for India alone, in charge of some 40 cases of "personal luggage" to shepherd to Darjeeling. Initially, the expedition would travel in two parties to avoid congestion in the dak bungalows where the sahibs would stay on route. The first division had left Darjeeling on May 18 with 50 mules, part of 100 loaned by the Government of India, 17 high-level porters (all Sherpas), two Lepcha porters, two cooks, and an orderly. The remaining men, mules, and another 22 porters took to the trail the following day.

Dr. Kellas was buried on a stony hillside overlooking the Tibetan plain, in view of the three great snow peaks he had climbed in Sikkim, and with Everest distantly visible to the west, more than a hundred miles away. Mallory found the small ceremony "extraordinarily affecting" and wrote to a friend, "I shan't easily forget the four boys, his own trained mountain-men, children of nature seated in wonder on a great stone near the grave, while Bury read out the passages from Corinthians."

As if the loss of Kellas were not enough, Raeburn too was exhibiting worryingly similar symptoms. Taking no chances, Wollaston decided to accompany him down to Lachen to recover. At a stroke, the team had lost three men and all its Himalayan experience. Yet, strangely, from this low point, spirits perked up. With Everest at last in sight, Mallory set himself to the task in hand, even renewing his efforts to get on well with Howard-Bury. "He is a keen mountaineer," he rationalized, "and a lover of flowers, so there must be some good in him," but added, "he can't turn Everest into his connoisseur's possession."

Thankfully, Mallory and Bullock got on well enough, for they were to work together throughout the reconnaissance, spending very few days out of each other's company. Bullock was placid, resilient, and a match for Mallory in stoicism. Morshead, too, quickly became a favorite, though his survey work kept him busy until well into July, when Mallory was delighted to see it dropped in favor of the climbing effort. Mallory did not hit it off so well with Wheeler whom he considered "a bore in the colonial fashion" and "a lame duck, suffering half the time from indigestion," on top of which "he grouses a good deal." But Heron proved a cheerful, jolly man, who helped keep an easy atmosphere going—"a solid treasure," admirable in running the men. To Geoffrey Young he wrote, "We're just about to walk off the map—the survey made from the Lhasa expedition. We've had one good distant view of Everest from above Kampa Dzong and I'm no believer in the easy north face. I hope we shall see him from 30-40 miles off from some slopes this (East) side of the Arun valley in the next week or so. Geoffrey, it's beginning to be exciting."

Mallory has described this initial good sighting of Everest, saying there could be no mistaking it or its neighbor: "That to the left must be Makalu, grey, severe, and yet distinctly graceful, and the other, away to the right—who could doubt its identity? It was a prodigious white fang excrescent from the jaw of the world." This choice of words clearly pleased Mallory, for they would crop up again in accounts of the next, and better, view that he and Bullock obtained of their goal some days later. Having crossed intervening ridges to reach the basin of the Arun River as it flowed south to cut through the Himalayan chain, they looked eagerly in the direction in case Makalu and Everest should reappear. "I felt somehow a traveller," Mallory wrote excitedly to Ruth. "It was not only that no European had ever been here before us, but we were penetrating a secret: we were looking behind the great barrier running north and south which had been as a screen in front of us ever since we turned our eyes westwards from Kampa Dzong." But the view was disappointingly blanketed in cloud. They decided to leave their ponies grazing and scramble up a little hill above Shilling in the hope this cloud would lift. After an hour's steep going they sat down with their field glasses to wait: "Suddenly our eyes caught glint of snow through the clouds; and gradually, very gradually, in the course of two hours or so, visions of great mountainsides and glaciers and ridges... forms invisible for the most part to the naked eye or indistinguishable from the clouds themselves, appeared through the floating rifts and had meaning for us—one whole clear meaning pieced from these fragments, for we had seen a whole mountain range, little by little, the lesser to the greater until, incredibly higher in the sky than imagination had ventured to dream, the top of Everest itself appeared."

The view continued to clear as they clambered down to regain their ponies and catch up with the baggage train. A stiff wind was blowing the sand and "all the landscape to the leeward was like a wriggling nightmare of watered silk." At sunset, established in their wayside camp, the wind dropped and, to the south, Everest rose "absolutely clear and glorious" in the fading light. No longer, Ruth was told, was it a mountain of fantasy. "The problem of its great ridges and glaciers began to take shape and to haunt the mind, presenting itself at odd moments and leading to definite plans."

Snow appears on the foothills as the expedition team fords a river that meanders along the Tibetan Plateau.

This was the east face of Mount Everest they were seeing, still over 50 miles away and with its lower slopes hidden, but already it was possible to make out that the long Northeast Ridge was not impossibly steep and that two notable cols separated the great mountain from its neighbors.

The spectacular fortress town of Shegar Dzong, with its whitewashed monastery buildings clinging like swallows' nests to the hillside, was reached on June 17. This regional capital boasted two *dzongpens*, or headmen, who were friendly and very helpful to the expedition; and a beautiful ceremonial tent was put at the team's disposal. Mallory and Bullock absented themselves from the main party for a couple of days for a side trip to the top of the Pang La, a magnificent viewpoint from which Everest dominates a horizon full of Himalayan giants.

Expedition headquarters were set up at Tingri village, a good supply base within a few day's reach of Everest. A large old Chinese rest

house, dilapidated and reputedly haunted, was put at the expedition's disposal. Here, Wollaston rejoined the party, having left Raeburn in Sikkim to recover, and from here the reconnaissance proper began. Mallory and Bullock set off at once to investigate Everest's northeastern approaches, while Wheeler and Heron went to Kyetrak to begin their surveys. Morshead and one of the two Indian survey assistants he'd brought with him, Gujhar Singh, explored northward and westward, leaving the other, Lalbir Singh, to complete plane-tabling in the vicinity. Howard-Bury set up a darkroom in one of the abandoned rooms—and almost gassed himself with the toxic fumes from his chemicals. Wollaston was anxious to get on with his natural-history collecting, but two of the native personnel were dangerously ill with typhoid fever, and he was obliged to turn one of the rest house's four courtyards into a hospital. In his diary, he grumbled that this was "the most filthy place for a camp imaginable." One of his patients, Wheeler's bearer, died despite his ministrations, but the other was tottering about within three weeks and, when well enough, was sent home to India. All the porters who were not out with the explorers were dispatched daily into the countryside to collect what specimens they could. Each evening a pile of carcasses—rats, lizards, birds, and beetles—were deposited at Wollaston's door. Later, he was able to resume his own collecting, though covertly, for fear of giving offense in a country whose Buddhist beliefs forbid the taking of life. He enjoyed successes, establishing, for instance, that the "whistling hare" was not a hare nor did it whistle, but was instead a marmotlike beast called a pika. Better still, one of his pika specimens yielded two different species of flea, both new to science.

Three days after leaving Tingri, Mallory and Bullock, with 16 of their best porters, trekked into the long, wind-scoured valley of the Rongbuk. The group was accompanied by the interpreter Gyalzen and 15 yaks, which replaced the baggage train of bullocks and donkeys. The Rongbuk was a bleak place, but that afternoon, as they surmounted a steep rise crowned by two chortens, they were stopped in their tracks. "A more glorious sight than I can attempt to describe," Mallory wrote to Ruth from their very first camp under Everest: "Suffice it to say that it has the most steep ridges and appalling precipices that I have ever seen, and that all the talk of an easy snow slope is a myth."

Like cowled figures in procession, the Central Rongbuk Glacier marches from the foot of Mount Everest. George Mallory climbed the nearby Ri-Ring to photograph the glacier on the team's first approach; upon returning to the bottom, he discovered that he had loaded the film incorrectly. So he climbed back up Ri-Ring for this dramatic shot.

Mallory knew he needed to describe the view from the camp for the expedition book: "At the end of the valley and above the glacier Everest rises not so much a peak as a prodigious mountain-mass," he wrote. "There is no complication for the eye. The highest of the world's great mountains, it seems, has to make but a single gesture of magnificence to be lord of all, vast in unchallenged and isolated supremacy. To the discerning eye other mountains are visible, giants between 23,000 and 26,000 feet high. No one of their slenderer heads even reaches their chief's shoulder; beside Everest they escape notice—such is the pre-eminence of the greatest."

With their tents pitched at 16,500 feet, just beyond the Rongbuk Monastery, not far from the Base Camp expeditions use today, the team began to explore their surroundings. Setting out at 3:25 a.m. on June 27, with Gyalzen and five porters, they made for the snout of the Main Rongbuk Glacier. There, with some difficulty, they crossed the issuing torrent to follow the right hand ("true left") bank of the glacier. At 7 a.m., when the sun at last reached them, they stopped for breakfast. Another hour's fast walking brought them to the confluence with the West Rongbuk Glacier, across which the Lingtren peaks blocked the view to the head of the main glacier. They intended to climb some distance up these attractive peaks to see further, but it was clear that the pace they were setting was exhausting the porters. They instead led their men across the maze of ice pinnacles that made up the main glacier. The ice formations reminded

Grim yet triumphant, the 1921 reconnaissance team included, from left (rear) Sandy Wollaston, Charles Howard-Bury, A.M. Heron, Harold Raeburn (front) Mallory, E. O. Wheeler, Guy Bullock, and H.T. Morshead.

Mallory of something out of *Alice in Wonderland* with their bewildering passages. It was a disconnected world of spires, chasms, and lakes, but he took heart from the apparent lack of lateral crevasses, supposing, rightly, that the spires were the result not so much of movement as of melting. Within an hour all were safely on the opposite ("true right") bank with no more damage than an inadvertent soaking for Mallory when he broke through the frozen surface of a small lake. "The loss of dignity perhaps was more serious than the chilling of ardour," he rationalized, and he soon dried out in the warm sun.

The last four miles back to camp was a "keen race against gathering darkness," It involved crossing another swollen stream, but Mallory was elated and pleased with his performance. "My darling," he wrote to Ruth, "this is a thrilling business altogether. I can't tell you how it possesses me, and what a prospect it is. And the beauty of it all!"

"I wish some folk at home could see the precipice on this side—a grim spectacle most unlike the long gentle snow slopes suggested by photos," he wrote the next day in his diary. "Amusing to think how one's vision of the last effort has changed; it looked like crawling half-blind up easy snow, an even slope all the way up from a camp on a flat snow shoulder; but it won't be that sort of grind; we'll want climbers

and not half-dazed ones; a tougher job than I bargained for. E. is a rock mountain."

Until August 18, when the Lhakpa La was reached, Mallory and Bullock tirelessly worked their way around the mountain, up glaciers and subsidiary peaks, establishing its full shape and difficulty. From an advance base camp close to the spot where they had breakfasted on the first day, Mallory investigated the upper basin of the Rongbuk Glacier and reported to Farrar that it ran itself "up into a cwm, like the Charge of the Light Brigade, up under a 10,000-foot precipice and...round the left towards something like the Col du Lion on the Tiefenmatten side [the North Col]." The North Ridge above the col appeared climbable, but how to surmount the North Col itself? Was its other side more promising? They would need to investigate, but first he and Bullock wanted to traverse into what they had called the "Western Cwm" to see what the mountain looked like on its Nepalese side. After various unsuccessful approaches, they finally managed to peer into this basin from the col between Lingtren and Pumori. To their disappointment the ground dropped steeply for 1,500 feet to the glacier. They were not sorry that this side was out of bounds in Nepal: An approach up the terribly steep and broken "Western Glacier" (the Khumbu Icefall) would have been daunting, and even were it possible, they doubted the "gap between Everest and the South Peak

[the South Col]" could be gained from there.

A question mark also hung over the "North West Ridge" (today, the West Ridge): If this were in the Alps, then perhaps the ridge might extend as far as its shoulder, but it was not an attractive prospect. By the second week in July, Mallory's optimism was wobbling, and he wrote to a climbing friend: "I sometimes think of this expedition as a fraud from beginning to end, invented by the wild enthusiasm of one man, Younghusband, puffed up by the would-be wisdom of certain pundits in the A. C. (Alpine Club); and imposed upon the youthful ardour of your humble servant...the prospect of ascent in any direction is almost nil, and our present job is to rub our noses against the impossible in such a way as to persuade mankind that some noble heroism has failed once again."

By now they were well into the monsoon season, and the second half of July brought fresh snow throughout the range. Any hopes of finding a high-level way to the east side of the mountain were abandoned—and with them Mallory's last chance of discovering the East Rongbuk Glacier, which would have provided an easier route to the northeast side of Everest. He and Bullock had realized there must be another large glacier on the far side of the North Col, but had not surmised that it curved around to find its outlet in the

Approaching Everest from the east, the team camped on Kharta Glacier at an elevation of 20,000 feet. From the summit of a 21,200 foot peak southwest of Advance Base Camp, George Mallory took this photograph of the imposing peaks of Chomolunzo and Makalu.

Rongbuk Valley. That the stream emerging from a side valley actually flowed from a major glacier to the east was only discovered later by Wheeler in the course of routine survey work in the valley.

Mallory and Bullock joined Howard-Bury at his new base camp at Kharta, which seemed idyllic and green after the barren Rongbuk. Mallory enjoyed a brief respite, writing to Ruth rhapsodically about the wildflowers, before taking up the struggle once more. He and Bullock set off with their porters to begin the eastern reconnaissance. Local people directed them toward Chomolungma, a route that seemed to be taking them too far south. It became clear that the Tibetans of this district knew two Chomolungmas and that the one for which they were heading must be Makalu. They could not be sorry: The scenery was staggering. Mallory's "vivid delight" at finding no less than three of the five highest summits in the world overlooking the Kama Valley, which they had now entered, left him speechless. Makalu, in particular was "incomparable for its spectacular and rugged grandeur."

At the broad end of the Kama Valley Everest rose, flanked on each side by its long ridges, the Northeast and the Southeast, curving round from Lhotse. On August 6 the party set up a camp to enable them to climb Kartse, a conical snowy summit on the watershed between the Kama Valley and the valley to the north of them, which was hoped to be the elusive basin beneath the North Col. That same night clouds lifted to reveal Everest rising from bright mists, "immanent, vast, incalculable—no fleeting apparition of elusive dream form: steadfast like Keats's star, in lone splendour hung aloft the night, diffusing, it seemed universally, an exalted radiance."

Before dawn the next morning they were climbing the slopes of Kartse, to the east of their mountain: "The white mountains were somehow touched to life by a faint blue light—a light that changed as the day grew, to a rich yellow on Everest and then a bright grey blue before it blazed all golden when the sun hit it, while Makalu, even more beautiful, gave us the redder shades, the flush of pink and purple shadows," Mallory wrote. "But I'm altogether beaten for words. The whole range of peaks from Makalu to Everest far exceeds any mountain scenery that I ever saw before."

They were afforded a good view of the great east face of Everest, spectacular in its architectural splendor, with massive buttresses of rock and ice dipping into the glacier beneath. Yet, it offered little comfort to the mountaineer. Practically the whole face was subject to falling ice from the formidable band of seracs above. "In short," Mallory wrote, "other men, less wise, might attempt this way if they would, but, emphatically, it was not for us."

The climb was steeper than they thought, and one by one the porters dropped out, but finally Mallory and a young lad named Nyima made it to the top. "And as the wind blew rifts in the snow I had glimpses of what I wanted to see, glimpses only, but enough to suggest a high snow cwm under this northeast face of Everest, finding its outlet somehow to the north." It now remained to find this outlet:

From the Kharta Glacier camp (above), the majestic sweep of Mount Everest offered no route to the summit, and left George Mallory dumbstruck by "the beauty of it all."

Searching for a route to the top, the reconnaissance team descends from Kartse at the head of the Kama Valley on August 7, 1921.

From Lhakpa La, Mallory spied what he was looking for: A reasonable route to the top of Everest. Across the basin (to the right in the panoramic image from the 1921 expedition) was the North Col of Everest, above which rises the North Ridge. Mallory wrote, "We have found out the way."

That would be their next task.

Up to this point Mallory and Bullock had been pleased with their performance. One or two of the porters had suffered a little from altitude, but the majority had grown stronger, as indeed had they themselves. Bullock had lost a lot of weight, but was now eating heartily. Mallory himself felt entirely well and optimistic, and thus was taken by surprise on his descent from Kartse to feel headachy and overcome by weariness. Once in camp, he couldn't stop shivering and spent a feverish night. For the better part of a week he remained under the weather, with what he supposed was tonsillitis—a sore throat and swollen glands. The team retreated to the Kharta Valley, where on August 11 they pitched a camp at 16,100 feet. Bullock explored alone until Mallory was well enough to continue. Time was running out. If a way was not found quickly to access the North Col from this side, it would be impossible to attempt a climb of Everest in September, as they all had hoped and planned.

The breakthrough came on August 18 when, joined by Morshead, they set off up the southern branch of the Kharta Glacier through snow so deep they had to wear snowshoes most of the day to save breaking through the surface up to their knees. It was misty and airless, and as the day wore on it felt like they were "walking in a white furnace," as Mallory wrote to Ruth. "Morshead, who knows the hottest heat of the plains of India, said that he had never felt any heat so intolerable as this." The pull up to the col at the end of the valley was fierce. But later in the day when the three men and the indefatigable Nyima finally stood on top of the Lhakpa La, the col that separated the Kharta Glacier from the East Rongbuk, they saw what they had long sought: "There sure enough was

the suspected glacier running north from the cwm under the north-east face of Everest," Mallory wrote to Ruth. "How we wished it had been possible to follow it down and find out the secret of its exit. There we were baffled. But the head of this glacier was only a little way below us, perhaps 700 feet at most, and across it lay our way, across easy snow up into the other side of the cwm, where the approach to the north col, the long wished-for goal, could not be difficult nor even long."

Mallory was overjoyed. At long last the reconnaissance had yielded a ray of hope. He couldn't wait to tell Ruth the news. "As we came down the long weary way, my thoughts were full of this prospect of success. I don't know when I have allowed myself so much enjoyment from a personal achievement. I fairly puffed out my chest with pride and the consciousness of something well done; of a supreme effort made and happily rewarded; of a big task accomplished. For this success brings our reconnaissance to an end, we have found out the way and we're now planning the attack."

It was only when he rejoined the main party in the Kharta Valley that Mallory learned the deflating news of Wheeler's discovery—of the course of this glacier, and its easier access from the main Rongbuk glacier. The news came too late to alter their plans. There was no time, nor the energy to move everyone and all their baggage back round to the Rongbuk.

Yet bad weather held up all activity for almost a month. Mallory and Bullock moved back to their advance base camp to await a break, where they were joined over the next few days by the others. Earlier in the expedition Mallory and Bullock had agreed that the chance of success for an Everest expedition was fifty to one against them in any one year. Now as time melted away, Mallory grew more despondent, telling Ruth that he no longer rated the odds higher than one in a thousand.

Then, "Wonder of wonders!" on the morning of September 16, "We just woke and found it different." At once they organized the porters to start ferrying loads. Four days later, after a cold night, Mallory and Morshead started moving men and stores up to Lhakpa La.

The snow was crisp underfoot to start, but higher up was worse than ever imagined. "No firm steps could be stamped by the leaders to save the coolies behind, and each in turn had to contend with the shifting substance of fine powder." Three porters fell out through exhaustion, another two loads had to be abandoned short of the pass, and the party straggled badly, but by the end of the day 11 loads were on the col. A camp was set up there, on the 22nd, tucked under the rim for shelter. "Each crawled into his hole," Mallory wrote to Geoffrey Young. "In a few minutes all was still. We were at very close quarters, 7 tents I think in the little shallow snow-basin; but hardly a remark passed from one to another. No cooking, no hand stirred for a thought of comfort; only rest, not sweet but deathlike, as though the spirit of the party had died within it."

All the porters were suffering in some degree from the effects of altitude and exertion, but ten were gathered the next day to accompany Mallory, Bullock, and Wheeler across the glacier basin. Another camp was placed in this hollow, which offered no protection from the fierce squalls that rattled the tents all night, threatening to tear them from their moorings.

The next morning, an hour or so after sunrise, they plodded off, up the steep slopes of the North Col with their three strongest porters. "Nothing very remarkable remains in my mind about the ascent...except perhaps Wheeler's

Ice ax in hand, Mallory trains porters in ice-climbing techniques. He and the rest of the team harbored some hope that they might actually climb Mount Everest as a finale to the reconnaissance mission, but it was now too late in the season. It was time to plan their return, and the first full-scale attempt to conquer Everest—shown in the following pages from the peak above Advance Base Camp.

black beard coming up behind me," Mallory reported later to Young. By 11:30 a.m. they were on the Col. And a gale was blowing ("the devil, dancing in a sudden tourbillon of snow which took away my breath"). Higher, unbroken spindrift blurred their view of the ridge, but the way looked feasible. For as far as they could see, the rock and snow slopes gave no indication of danger nor difficulty. Were they fresher and the wind less violent, Mallory was sure this route could lead them to the summit, but to go on now would be madness. They struggled a few more steps to put the matter to the test but, exposed to the full force of the wind, quickly scuttled back below the lip of the Col. Nothing more was said about pushing the assault further.

To Ruth he wrote at the earliest opportunity, "I am well in spite of all efforts and disappointment. It is a disappointment, there is no getting over it, that the end should seem so much tamer than I hoped. But...I doubt if any big mountain venture has ever been made with a smaller margin of strength. I carried the whole party on my shoulders to the end, and we were turned back by a wind in which no man could live for an hour.... As it is we have established the way to the summit for anyone who cares to try the highest adventure."

CLIMBING THE NORTH RIDGE DURING THE 1922 EXPEDITION MALLORY (LEFT) AND MAJ. E. F. NORTON, APPROACH THEIR RECORD-SETTING HIGH POINT OF 26,985 FEET.

CHAPTER THREE

We were deplorably tired... .Knees did not always bend and unbend as required. At times they gave way all together.... Weak from hunger and exhausted by that nightmare struggle for life, we were in no fit condition to proceed.

GEORGE FINCH, 1922

THE KNEES OF THE GODS

Mallory struggled with a sense of failure during the long journey home. He was desperate to see Ruth and the children; seven months was a long time to be away. He found himself yearning for calm and familiar scenes—"Bloomsbury in a fog...cattle grazing in western meadows...." On the boat from Bombay, he kept largely to his cabin, writing furiously. Letters to friends, a report for Younghusband, an article for the journals of the Alpine Club and Royal Geographical Society, the talk he would give at the joint meeting of these two bodies, his contribution to the planned expedition book—he went over and over the events of the reconnaissance and the attempt, working out his disappointment, reconciling "visions of myself with a few determined spirits setting forth from our perched camp on that high pass, crawling up at least to a much higher point where the summit itself would seem almost within reach, and coming down tired but not dispirited, satisfied rather, just with the effort," and the reality as he had found it—"the blown snow, endlessly swept over the grey slopes, just the grim prospect, no respite and no hope."

As he approached Marseilles, where Ruth had traveled to meet him, he felt easier in his mind. The overwhelming emotion now, he told Geoffrey Young, was of relief that he hadn't been tempted to go further. "We came back without accident, not even a frostbitten toe. It seems now a question not as to what might have happened higher, but what would have happened with unfailing certainty. It was a pitiful party at the last, not fit to be on a mountainside anwhere." And, to David Pye, he wrote: "When I think of that wonderful Everest Committee and all the solemn divergences of opinion that must have passed between their nodding heads, the scrutiny of photographs and discussion of letters, with grave doubts coughed up in phlegmy throats as to whether the party are really 'on the right track,' and all the anxious wisdom devoted to spoon-feeding the Glaxo-loving public—lord, when I think of it, something bubbles up inside me. The effervescence is sternly repressed, of course. I settle down to pondered judgements; and then—a bubble outs and bursts."

One thing they had learned was that the best time of attack was probably before the monsoon, which would mean arriving at base camp in April. Mallory couldn't imagine how another expedition could be put together in time for the following year. At least eight first-rate climbers would be required; where would they come from? To his sister Avie he said that when the committee pressed him for an answer, he'd tell them to find the other seven first. "I wouldn't go again next year," he told her, "for all the gold in Arabia."

There was no prospect of reward, of course, but he had no job to return to either. In the end, once it was clear that the next expedition would have General Bruce as leader and include "real climbers" in its ranks, Mallory found he could not pass up the opportunity. He would spend three months in England, then return east to take up the struggle once again.

This time, George Ingle Finch would join the party. Bullock could not come—in fact the only person from 1921 who would return with Mallory was Morshead, but in the capacity of climber, not surveyor. There would be no topographical work in 1922. Disquiet had been expressed in official circles over a careless remark that the 1921 survey was a "military" reconnaissance. Even A. M. Heron, who was intent on completing his geological survey, was turned back at the last moment because his rock-collecting last year disturbed the "dragons" that live under the sacred mountains. In any event, 12,000 square miles of quarter-inch original survey work had been completed by the 1921 team, and a further one thousand square miles in Sikkim revised; Wheeler completed a detailed photo survey of 600 square miles of the environs of Mount Everest, advance copies of which would catch up with the 1922 party en route.

The other climbers would be Maj. Edward "Teddy" Norton, a great sportsman and naturalist; doctors Howard Somervell and Arthur Wakefield, both from the English Lake District; and two senior Alpine Club members, Col.

On its 1922 approach march, the team had to ford a river on the Tibetan Plateau. Arthur Wakefield (center at right) took off his boots to keep them dry. Howard Somervell (left) did him one better by removing his trousers. Mallory (right) wondered why they were being so timid.

Mealtimes were a formal affair, with expedition members sitting at tables and chairs. General Bruce, leader of the expedition, presides at the head.

Returning to the hillside town of Shegar Dzong, the expedition once more made camp on the dry plain. Curious Tibetans peeked into the climbers' tents, dazzled by the exotic array of equipment brought to tackle the slopes of Mount Everest.

Edward Strutt, as the expedition's second-in-command, and Tom Longstaff, as surgeon and naturalist. Joining in India would be the general's cousin, Capt. Geoffrey Bruce, as well as Capt. C. J. Morris—both from Gurkha regiments—and Colin Crawford of the Indian Civil Service: All these spoke local languages and would assist with overland travel arrangments. A prodigious photographic outfit was arranged under the direction of Capt. John Noel who was supplied with three cinematograph cameras; two panoramic cameras, of which one rotated through the complete circle; four cameras for glass plates (one of large format); one stereoscopic camera; and five Vestpocket Kodaks. He brought darkroom equipment for developing films in the field.

British society in the 1920s was rigidly stratified, and people were inevitably categorized according to rank or profession, so it is no surprise that Arthur Hinks, secretary to the Everest Committee and editor of *The Geographical Journal,* announced with pride: "Of the eleven members of the expedition six are soldiers: three of the Gurkhas, one of the Royal Scots,

one Royal Field Artillery, and one machine Gun Corps, formerly of the East Yorkshire Regiment. Three members of the party are of Cambridge University: Mr. Mallory of Magdalene, Mr. Somervell of Caius, and Dr. Wakefield of Trinity. Two are of Oxford University: Colonel Strutt and Dr. Longstaff, both of Christ Church. Three are surgeons; two are naturalists; several are expert photographers; one at least is a painter; and all are distinguished mountaineers. It is, in fact, a very strong party, of which much is expected."

Without leaving his desk at the Royal Geographical Society offices, Hinks was closely involved with all the British-launched expeditions to Everest prior to the Second World War. Dealing with the day-to-day correspondence, he had a finger in every stage of the planning, was the first to read and disseminate the expedition bulletins, and, as a gifted cartographer, tried to reconcile conflicting geographical data in advance of the mapping results. He was quite prepared to act on his own initiative and beyond his authority, which suited the committee as long as things went well and smoothly. But he could be a loose cannon and wrap his own prejudices and outspoken criticisms into a royal "we," giving the impression that these views were shared by the committee as a whole. He certainly got caught up in the excitement of the Everest struggle, but initially had little patience with mountaineers or mountaineering, which he considered frivolous compared to scientific work or photography. In particular, he clashed frequently with his Alpine Club counterpart, Percy Farrar, who could be a match for Hinks in obstinacy.

Historians owe Hinks a great debt: He was a meticulous record-keeper. Every piece of paper that crossed his desk was filed, with the result that the Royal Geographical Society, which has inherited the pictures and paperwork of the Mount Everest Committee, not only holds a unique collection of topographical photographs taken in these exploratory years, but also has a time capsule of documents, invoices, committee notes, clippings, papers returned from India, letters to and from almost all the early Everesters as well as from members of the general public—papers enough to fill scores of boxes and files. And the detail is astounding. In those days, when postal deliveries were made three or more times a day and a note could cross London in a matter of hours, discussions tended to take place on paper, rather than over the telephone. From Hinks' collection, it is possible to follow all the arguments and heart-searching behind selecting equipment and team members. It is a priceless legacy.

Mallory reported to Ruth what a jolly and congenial party it was this year, and what a contrast to Charles Howard-Bury they had in Bruce, whose cheery character was as generous as his outline. On the little train to Darjeeling, with his head out of the window most of the time,

Meeting with Shegar Dzong's dzongpen *(second from right), the district's civil leader, from left, Mallory, Norton, and Geoffrey Bruce discussed their adventure. The group brought gifts to present to dzongpen in each district they passed through.*

the general was "brimming over with joy and waving his handkerchief to passers by."

Bruce had waited nearly 30 years to fulfill his dream of going to Everest. The robust health of his youth had been eroded by long service in India, vicious bouts of malaria, and assorted battle scars. He was invalided out of the Army in 1919 suffering "cardiac debility with great enlargement." Doctors, he used to say, told him to go home and lead a quiet life, "...scarcely any organ in my body remained unaffected. Even my liver was found to be so large that it required two men and a boy to carry it." Luckily, he found a climber-doctor who told him his best way to keep fit was mild mountaineering, and it worked. In 1921 he was allowed to climb as much as he wanted in the Alps and returned very fit.

Younghusband once described Bruce as "an extraordinary mixture of boy and man," remarking that "you never know which of them you are talking to." Bruce perpetually effervesced with boyish fun, but was shrewd, competent, and would not stand the slightest nonsense—it was an effective combination. His expansiveness and boisterous humor was treated with suspicion by Hinks, who worried that he was spending expedition funds like water. How could Bruce need 500 mules to get all the equipment on the road, he would grumble. "Captain Noel will be arriving at Darjeeling with a box 40 feet long," Bruce

told him, "and I am currently scouring the country for an adequate mule."

It amused Morshead to hear Bruce dictating his dispatches to Morris on the expedition typewriter. "The other day, in a letter to the R.G.S. he remarked that he had done 'everything possible to help the expedition forward, from interviewing the Viceroy to emptying the poes in a *dak* bungalow,'" he told his wife. "Can you imagine old Hinks, who hasn't a grain of humor in his composition, rubbing his gold-rimmed spectacles in amazement as he reads out Bruce's dispatches to the assembled committee?!"

The trek to base camp followed more or less the route reconnoitered in 1921, but being two months earlier in the year it was colder too; the men walked to keep warm, riding their horses only when exhausted. At night they would wrap themselves in their layers of clothing. From Phari to Kampa Dzong they tried the shorter route, but encountered deep snow and a howling wind. The nagging suspicion that Kellas might have been saved if they'd come this way last time was dispelled. They visited his grave, adding a few stones to its cairn.

At Kampa, Finch and Crawford caught up with the party, having been delayed by the late arrival of the oxygen equipment. Finch wasted no time in making sure all the climbers were familiar with its workings, and instigated daily oxygen drills. "An interesting entertainment," Mallory called it, which "showed up several weaknesses which had developed in the apparatus.... Nothing that is incapable of adjustment, but showing only too well how many chances are against its working properly." He could not get over his distaste of one procedure, which involved holding a rubber tube in the mouth. "I sicken with the thought of the saliva dribbling down," he confided to Ruth.

Beyond Kampa, the weather got warmer, but several team members developed colds and flu-like symptoms. Longstaff was feeling so poorly at Tinki Dzong that they took an extra rest day to help him regain his strength. The old gentleman appeared alarmingly frail and did not really have the physique for this sort of life.

On leaving Shegar Dzong, they crossed over the Pang La and tramped into Rongbuk on the last day of April. On May Day, "punctual to programme," Bruce delivered his caravan of around 160 men "burly and fit" to within a mile of the snout of the main glacier where base camp was set up in full view of Everest. That night they drank to his health with champagne.

In approaching the North Col by the shorter route of the East Rongbuk Glacier, the party's priority was to work out where campsites should be placed along the 12-mile route to advance base camp at the glacier head, below the steep slopes of the col. Strutt, with most

Captain Noel's hand-tinted photograph of a Tibetan ceremonial tent at the foot of the monastery at Shegar was aimed at exciting the imagination of audiences at home. Mallory and others from the team gave frequent lectures, often illustrated with lantern slide images from the expeditions.

experience at reading snow and ice conditions, was sent to reconnoiter the route and took Longstaff, Morshead, and Norton with him. "An ideal party, full of energy and experience and not too young," he said. "Morshead and Norton are blessed with the sweetest tempers and dispositions, while Longstaff and I, who are gifted with just the reverse, were able, on the strength of a friendship of many year's standing, to curse each other freely and without malice."

Bruce had hoped to use yaks above Base Camp, perhaps as high as Advance Base—which is where these animals go to today—but he found their drivers unwilling to risk them on the trackless, rugged moraines. Stores and equipment would need to be transported by local porters in order to preserve the energies of the hand-picked Nepalese porters for higher altitudes. Unfortunately, it was ploughing season in Tibet, and few villagers could be coaxed to spend more than a day or two working for the expedition. Nevertheless a steady stream of short-term local carriers was forthcoming—"a motley throng of old men, women, boys and girls," Wakefield wrote, adding, "To ensure that none of them dropped or dumped anything en route and then came back claiming full pay, Morris and I were detailed to follow behind, keeping the flock together and preventing stragglers. We were instructed not to hurry them. I felt like a Westmorland farmer driving a flock to market. At 18,000 feet—how these coolies carried their loads completely puzzles me! Some were 80 pounds!" Some of the women were carrying babies as well, and all would sleep out under rocks at 16 or 17,000 feet where temperatures dipped well below freezing, the watercourses frozen solid.

Mallory knew the basin at the head of the East Rongbuk; Wheeler had surveyed a length from its other end, but no one had yet ascended the full course of the glacier. "It was a strange and weird world that Strutt and his companions entered," wrote Younghusband in his history of Everest exploration. "The glacier in its middle section was eroded into the most fantastic icy pinnacles, flotillas of them, sailing down like giant yachts, up to a hundred feet high, dazzling and glistening in the sun."

An excellent site was found for Camp I at 17,800 feet on a pebbly terrace, not far into the East Rongbuk valley. Stone walls were thrown up and roofed with canvas tarpaulins to give additional room and shelter. Camp II was 2,000 feet higher, a three-hour journey, and spectacularly set beside a cliff of ice. Captain Noel, in his film and writings, called this "Frozen Lake Camp." Advance Base, Camp III, was pitched on moraine at 21,300 feet under the shelter of the North Peak, a bleak, cold spot—Noel's "Snowfield Camp," where night temperature often dropped below zero. Longstaff's efforts on the glacier took the stuffing out him. To his acute embarrassment ("Oh, the disgrace of it!"), he had to be carried back to base on a litter, and was effectively out of action for the rest of the expedition. Wakefield diagnosed "influenza, laryngitis, pharyngitis and tracheitis, and very weak." Morshead wrote to his wife, "I'm horribly afraid of another Kellas case, unless the General insists on his staying down at base.

Base Camp was established at 16,500 feet. The level, grassy terrain and abundant water supply made for an ideal camp.

Then began the task of creating the team's home away from home: Erecting tents, unpacking supplies, organizing the warm clothes and breathing apparatus they would use in the assault on Everest.

The climbing team was vastly outnumbered by the porters, who were hired according to three grades: Those who transported goods and equipment to Base Camp; those who helped supply camps further up the mountain; and an elite dozen or so talented and fit enough to handle duties at the very highest elevations.

It's a pity that people cannot learn that Himalayan mountaineering is a young man's game; I'm going to give it up myself when I'm 40!"

Cooks were installed in all camps and throughout that month, stores and oxygen supplies were ferried up the glacier—"up the line" as the team called it in a hangover from their war days. Mallory and Somervell left Base on May 10 with the idea of pushing beyond Camp III, up the North Col; and establishing a camp on its crest. Younghusband, describing this, has stressed the error, as he saw it, of sending two such strong mountaineers up high so early. These men were "the very pick of the whole party" and should have been "kept in clover at the Base, or in one of the glacier camps, exercising and acclimatizing...but always having a comfortable camp to return to." By leaving the drudgery to others and waiting till the way was "all smooth," they could have passed rapidly and comfortably through and been in the best possible condition for making the supreme effort upon which all else depended. "That is what theoretically should have been done," he said, "But again, theory had to be abandoned."

The dangerous slopes of the North Col required a quite different ascent line from the

autumn before, and more crevasses had opened up on top. The huddle of tents making up Camp IV occupied an icy shelf just below the rim. This was Noel's "Ice Cliff Camp," to which stores were now being ferried up. Strutt, in charge of the climbing effort, felt the time had come for "a full-dress reconnaissance."

Almost everyone except Bruce, Morshead, and Wakefield had been suffering stomach troubles to some degree. Mallory's was slight and he expected to be over it soon, but Finch had been confined to bed for several days. "A poor way of training for a high climb," Morshead remarked. The original plan for an oxygenless attempt by Mallory and Somervell, to be followed by one comprising Finch and Norton using oxygen, was another theory abandoned. With Finch laid low, and fears that the monsoon could be upon them soon, Mallory, Somervell, Norton, and Morshead took nine porters up the North Col, pitched five more tents and slept there. They would set off early the next day, up the arête of the North Ridge, taking the first steps ever on the mountain proper.

Mallory wrote to Ruth the night before this attempt, telling her, "I shall feel happier, in case of difficulties, to think that I have sent you a message of love." He doubted the difficulties ahead would provide many surprises; the unknown factors were the limits of their own endurance and will to go on. "It's all on the knees of the gods, and they are bare cold knees." He signed off, "Dearest one, you must know that the spur to do my best is you and you again.

In moments of depression or lack of confidence or overwhelming fatigue, I want more than anything to prove worthy of you. All my love to you. Many kisses to Clare and Berridge and John."

The plan was to establish Camp V at a height of around 27,000 feet, taking along two "Mummery" tents, sleeping bags, some provisions and cooking utensils; and then to send the porters back down, hopefully all the way to III. As the sun left the mountain at 4:30 p.m., they lay in their sacks on the col, with their thermos flasks filled beside them, ready for the morning meal. To Mallory, their prospects seemed "extraordinarily promising."

He was up at five to rouse the others, only to find the porters reluctant to stir. All were suffering the effects of altitude, and only five were fit enough to accompany them. A further delay as they thawed out their tins of spaghetti for breakfast, which had inadvertently been left out in the snow, made it 7 o'clock before the little group was away. Morshead set the pace. Any hopes that the day would warm up were soon dashed when a cold breeze sprang up from the west. The climbers put on all their spare clothes—except Morshead, who delayed disastrously.

The porters, not so well equipped, were growing colder the higher they went. It became clear to Mallory that he needed to rethink their plans. Strenuous step-cutting in hard snow had left them exhausted, and they were glad to stop around midday in the lee of some rocks at

The goal was ever in sight from Base Camp: Everest's North Face loomed against the dark sky some 12 miles away. Jetstream winds from the west scour the summit, creating a plume of mist that has become the mountain's trademark.

Despite the cold, the blazing sun of Everest's high elevations—here at Camp II—could burn the skin and cause snowblindness. Team members used umbrellas, goggles, and zinc oxide for protection from its powerful rays.

about 25,000 feet. There could be no question of going higher. Traversing around on the sheltered, east side of the ridge, one precarious tent platform was fashioned from stacked stones, and a steeply tilted slab, 50 yards away, served as another. "No more uncomforable arrangement could have been devised," Mallory wrote of the latter. The tent's two occupants rolled on top of each other all night, into the sharp rocks at the lower edge of the slab.

The porters were glad to be off and scuttled back to the col. The climbers were already suffering from the effects of the cold, and fortunately the night was mild, not below 7°F. The most seriously affected was Morshead. "Too late in the day he had put on his sledging suit for protection against the wind," Mallory wrote. "On arriving in camp he was chilled and evidently unwell." To make matters worse, Norton's rucksack containing spare warm clothing for the night had been lost when it slipped from his knee during a rest stop and fell all the way down the mountain.

The wind dropped, and at intervals during the night stars were visible, seeming to promise a better day ahead. As dawn approached, however, Mallory was disgusted to observe that the ground outside was white. "A little later," he wrote, "listening, we heard fine hail falling on the tents, and peering out of the tent door it was possible to make out that the cloud and mist were coming up from the east on a monsoon current." By 6:30 a.m., conditions were slightly improved and they began again the pantomime of preparing breakfast in awkward conditions. Another rucksack was dropped and bounded down the mountain. This one contained precious provisions and would have been a disastrous loss, had it not lodged on a ledge some hundred feet below them. "Morshead," Mallory tells us, "with heroic exertions, recovered it." The effort all but finished him off. As they were about to set off up the mountain once more, at around 8 o'clock, Morshead announced, "I think I won't come with you. I am quite sure I shall only keep you back."

Disappointed, the others, all still muzzy with headache after the poor night, pressed on without him. The snow obscured ledges and loose stones, obstructing progress. Though the ground could not be described as difficult, Mallory observed that all the little ledges of which it was composed, "tilted disadvantageously," requiring care and good balance. They kept close to the ridge, heading toward the Northeast Shoulder. However deeply they drew breath, progress was little more than "a miserable crawl," but all three seemed equally matched. By 2 p.m. it became clear that they could not reach the shoulder, still some 500 feet above, if they were to get Morshead down to the safety of the North Col that night. "And in any case," Mallory reported later to the Joint Meeting of the Royal Geographical Society and Alpine Club. "It would have been an insane risk to climb to the utmost limit of one's strength on Mount Everest and trust to inspiration or brandy to get one down in safety; for the body does not recover strength in the descent as it does in the Alps."

At 2:15 p.m., they turned back, with sufficient strength in reserve, they believed, for the long task ahead. None of them felt too badly about not going on; exertion robbed them of feeling much at all. When they had started out from the North Col the world altitude record for a climber stood at 24,600 feet; this day's efforts had raised it to 26,985 feet.

Stopping only to pick up Morshead and a few essential items, they left tents and sleeping bags where they were and headed back the way they'd come. The fresh coating of snow had obliterated the trail and made the once-easy ground slick and slippery. In places it was necessary to cut steps. They roped together, Mallory leading for most of the way, except when Norton took a share of the step-cutting. As he wrote to Ruth a few days afterward, he was feeling "pretty strong" on the descent. It was well that he was alert. "I hadn't realised then how shaky Morshead was and had cut rather poor steps; but there was good holding for the pick," Mallory reported. "Norton and Somervell must have been caught napping. I hadn't the rope belayed round my axe, as I was on the point of cutting a step, but, hearing something wrong behind, drove in my pick and belayed and was ready in plenty of time when the strain came."

Some likened them to sailing ships, others to shark's teeth, but the ice pinnacles of East Rongbuk Glacier, near Camp II, were a constant source of amazement to team members, who often wandered off to explore them. In this hand-tinted photograph by Noel, they may show a bit more blue than in real life.

In the vast expanse of East Rongbuk Glacier, John Morris is barely visible as he brings porters to Camp II.

All three had fallen, to be held on the rope by Mallory. Badly shaken, they proceeded with the utmost caution, Morshead by this time was so ill that he could only manage a few steps at a time. As the angle eased, Norton was able to support Morshead, while Mallory scouted ahead and Somervell acted as rearguard. Lightning flickered through the gathering gloom.

Their camp on the North Col was situated among the crevasses at the far end, toward Changtse. It was a tricky place to reach in daylight, let alone in near-darkness. A glimmer of starlight lit the crevasses, and Somervell produced a candle-lantern from his rucksack, which they managed to light on about the 12th match. "By its light," wrote Mallory, "we groped hither and thither to find our way." By sheer providence none fell through the concealed crevasses before reaching the edge of a little cliff, some 15 feet high. This, they had to jump down, an alarming prospect in the dark, but accomplished it safely. A fixed rope that would lead them back to their tents lay buried, and the last candle guttered out. "We groped for some time along the edge of the precipice and then began to go down at a steep angle, doubting whether this were the way. Suddenly someone hooked up the rope. We knew then that we could reach the tents."

It is often said of George Ingle Finch that it was his misfortune to be the right age to attempt Mount Everest in the 1920s. He would have been more at home a generation or more later when expeditions paid attention to the role of science and technology in overcoming physical obstacles and human limitations. At the start he had no

strong opinions one way or another about using additional oxygen to assist climbing at high altitude, but his work with Professor Dreyer had completely converted him. Notwithstanding the weight and complication of the oxygen apparatus, its employment, he now believed, was both essential and logical. No climber would reach the top without it, and to consider it an "artificial" aid he felt was the result of slipshod thinking. "The mountaineer conserves as far as possible his animal heat by wearing specially warm clothing," he would argue. "If science could prepare oxygen in tabloid form or supply it to us in thermos flasks that we might imbibe it like our hot tea, the stigma of 'artificiality' would, perhaps, be effectively removed. But when it has to be carried in special containers, its whole essence is held to be altered, and by using it the mountaineer is taking a sneaking, unfair advantage of the mountain!"

In his thinking and in his manner, Finch was out of sync with his companions. And, from the way he had been arbitrarily dropped from the team the previous year, he was aware his presence this time was not universally welcomed. He felt an outsider, and it did not make camp-life easy.

Finch had come in for his share of leg-pulling on the journey over for the oxygen drills to which he subjected his fellows. Mallory had remarked that it was fantastic nonsense to think one needed a fortnight's training to understand the apparatus: Two days would be ample. We can assume the sentiment was shared, for one day on the boat Finch was presented with a poem, written by his mutinous pupils—it included such verses as:

The weather was fine and we all were at ease
And prepared for a fortnight's good rest on the seas.

But Hark? What is that? It's six bells without doubt
And soon all our holiday's gone up the spout,
For whether we're resting, or reading or ill
We're ruthlessly summoned to Oxygen Drill.

The drills were then abandoned until traveling across Tibet, where they met with little more enthusiasm. The committee wanted the apparatus to be put fully to the test on the mountain, and Bruce, to his credit, made sure supplies were stacked and ready at advance base camp. Even so, he was no enthusiast, confessing that the apparatus "rather terrified" him. It seemed altogether too liable to be damaged by hitting or catching its tubing against rocks, and the change of bottles on steep slopes could be a tricky procedure for weary men.

When, ill in his sleeping bag at base camp on May 14, Finch saw all the fit climbers—the first assault party—"going up the line" together and realized that the second, gas attempt planned for himself and Norton would never take place, his spirits crashed. One characteristic he shared with Mallory, however, was a "purpose unhoneycombed with half-heartedness." His scientific work still needed doing; he still wanted his chance at the mountain. However, the odds had changed, he was not to be reckoned as out of it yet.

As soon as he was well, Finch looked around for companions to share his task. It was an easy enough choice. First, there was Geoffrey Bruce, the General's young cousin: "Tall, of athletic build, strong, endowed with a great fund of mental energy—an invaluable asset on ventures of this kind—and cheerful in any

Camp III, also called Advance Base Camp—from which the actual attempt to reach the summit would be launched—was established at 21,300 feet. Gathered around a meal of commercial canned foods are, from left, climbing leader Edward Strutt, A. W. Wakefield, H. T. Morshead, Teddy Norton, Howard Somervell, and George Mallory.

situation." Bruce regrettably had never in his life done any mountaineering. Next, Finch considered one of the Gurkha non-commissioned officers attached to the expedition, a tall, deep-chested young man with a grin almost as broad as his shoulders. On the principle that "the man who grins most, is usually the one who goes farthest in the mountains" Lance-Corporal Tejbir was selected to strengthen the party. Gathering what porters they could, these three now moved up the line.

Three days were spent at Camp III preparing apparatus and making important adjustments to it. Out came the hacksaws, pliers, and soldering iron. The modified apparatus was tested on a trip to the Rapiu La at the foot of the long Northeast Ridge. Toward sunset on the 21st the four members of the first climbing party could be seen descending the North Ridge toward Camp IV. The next morning Finch led his party and Wakefield out to meet them on the lower slopes of the Col, observing, "They were obviously in the last stages of exhaustion, as indeed men should be who had done their best on a mountain like Everest." He did not consider they could recover sufficiently for another attempt and, after passing over thermoses of hot tea and entrusting them to Wakefield's care, he continued up the Col. This was another trial run

for the oxygen, and he was delighted at the speed they made. He suspected some of their Sherpas, too, were coming round to the idea that this "English Air" really did have therapeutic effects.

On the 24th, Finch was at last ready and took his men back up to the North Col. The next morning their porters were away up the North Ridge by 8 a.m., and they followed an hour and a half later. Finch, Bruce, and Tejbir were all carrying 30-pound loads, more than the average porter load, yet, sucking oxygen, they had caught up to the others by the time they reached 24,500 ft.

Finch was anxious to camp higher than Mallory's party had done—at 26,000 feet. He had to settle for 500 feet less, as the afternoon brought stiff winds. Before sending back the porters, a little platform was leveled out on the backbone of the ridge, an exposed spot, with slopes falling away to the East Rongbuk and Main Rongbuk glaciers on either side. It began to snow and, later, a gale blew up. Gusts tore at the little tent, threatening to tear it from its moorings. Sleep was out of the question as they fought to hang on to their flimsy shelter.

The fierce winds did not abate until around 1 p.m. the following day. Finch was delighted that his companions *(continued on page 108)*

OXYGEN ON EVEREST

Eminent scientists in 1922 were by no means convinced that Everest could be climbed without the aid of supplemental oxygen. Balloonists had been known to collapse and die at lesser altitudes. "If you do succeed," the Everest Committee was warned by Professor Dreyer, a consultant physiologist for the Royal Air Force, "you may not get down again." Accordingly, an oxygen subcommitte was set up by the Alpine Club, comprising Capt. Percy Farrar, George Finch, Howard Somervell, and another climber-scientist, P. J. H. Unna. They were to study the problem and to order whatever equipment was necessary. In Professor Dreyer's pressure chamber in Oxford, Finch and Somervell underwent tests that took them to a simulated height of 23,000 feet. They were required to step on and off a chair with a 35-pound load. Finch managed with no apparent difficulty, but Somervell appeared to waver after his fifth step. He vigorously denied that he felt any ill effects, but his insistence was taken as a sign that he was exhibiting the quarrelsome characteristics known to be one symptom of hypoxia (oxygen deficiency), and oxygen was forcibly administered.

It is not the proportion of oxygen in the air that diminishes as climbers gain elevation—this remains a constant 20.93 per cent—but the atmospheric pressure that decreases. At 18,000 feet it is only half that at sea level and at the summit of Everest it falls to a third that at sea level. The body has trouble making the necessary gaseous exchanges in the lungs at diminished pressures like these. The first indication of oxygen deprivation will be an increased respiratory rate, as the climber strains after usable air. The heartbeat quickens to 140 beats per minute or more, making exercise extremely difficult; even rolling over in your sleeping bag leaves you breathless for many minutes afterward. The blood thickens, making you more susceptible to thrombosis and strokes, and it turns a very dark red, so that the face and hands appear bluish in color—especially the finger nails. As unconsciousness approaches, there may be mental confusion and irritability, and the blueness becomes even more marked.

1922 OXYGEN APPARATUS; TOP: 1924 OXYGEN BOTTLE

These days we understand more about such altitude disorders as pulmonary or cerebral edema and other circulatory problems, but in the 1920s this knowledge was rudimentary. Climbers, and porters, exhibiting symptoms were often misdiagnosed. The reason for taking supplemental oxygen was to enhance performance and allow humans to penetrate thinner atmospheres. Dr. Alexander Kellas had carried out some useful research into mountain sickness and made initial, inconclusive experiments with artificial oxygen, but before the pioneering Everest expeditions little was known about the body's own natural defense mechanism—acclimatization.

Announcing that oxygen equipment would be taken by the 1922 expedition, Secretary Arthur Hinks betrayed his scepticism over its worth. "A section of the climbers had convinced themselves," he wrote, "or had been convinced that they would never reach the summit without it. The Committee, feeling bound to supply whatever in reason might be demanded, cheerfully faced the large expenditure required." He poked fun at the equipment and at the complicated procedures devised for laying out bottles to assure sufficient supplies were provided at stages on the climbers' way up the mountain. Captain Farrar was furious with him. "I will say quite frankly that I do not like the somewhat satirical tone of your article," he told Hinks. "You will be seen as a doubter." Hinks, unrepetent, retorted, "If some of the party do not get to 25,000 to 26,000 feet without oxygen, they will be rotters."

GEOFFREY BRUCE, 1922

Oxygen was no more an artifical aid than food, in Farrar's opinion. The human frame was attuned to a certain quantity of it, and all the subcommittee was trying to do was to maintain that supply. Moreover, he told Hinks, "I start with the strong conviction that, whatever they do, no party in similar conditions could do more."

The chief advocate for supplemental oxygen was George Ingle Finch, who had been designated the team's oxygen officer. Certainly the equipment was unpopular with many of the climbers, who had difficulty accepting it as either legitimate or aesthetic. Climbing was about man versus mountain, not man and technology forcing a mountain into submission. Besides, as Mallory said, climbing with such a weight and a mask over one's face held little charm. Finch did not feel strongly one way or another to start with, but his work with Dreyer completely converted him. Its weight and complication notwithstanding, he now believed

OXYGEN DRILL DURING THE 1922 APPROACH MARCH

the apparatus to be both essential and logical. To consider it an "artificial" aid was in his opinion the result of slipshod thinking: "The mountaineer conserves as far as possible his animal heat by wearing specially warm clothing," he would argue. "No one demurs; it is the common-sense thing to do. He pours his hot tea from a thermos bottle—and never blushes! Without fear of adverse criticism, he doctors up his inside with special heat and energy-giving foods and stimulants! From the sun's ultra-violet rays and the wind's bitter cold, he boldly dares to protect his eyes with Crookes' anti-glare glasses; further, he wears boots that to the average layman look ridiculous! The use of caffeine to supply just a little more buck to an almost worn-out human frame is not cavilled at despite its being a synthetic drug the manufacture of which involves the employment of complicated plant and methods. If science could prepare oxygen in tabloid form or supply it to us in thermos flasks that we might imbibe it like our hot tea, the stigma of 'artificiality' would, perhaps, be effectively removed. But when it has to be carried in special containers, its whole essence is held to be altered, and by using it the mountaineer is taking a sneaking, unfair advantage of the mountain!"

It was not as if, by the inhalation of a little life-giving gas, the climber smoothed away the rough rocks of the mountain nor stilled the storm; nor was he wafted by invisible agents to his goal. No, Finch declared, "Oxygen renders available more of his store of energy and so hastens his steps, but it does not, alas! fit the wings of Mercury to his feet."

All the same, by the time Base Camp was reached in 1922, Finch knew himself to be "almost alone in my faith in oxygen." He was even more discouraged when he and a novice mountaineer, Geoffrey Bruce, climbed high with the controversial gas, and their achievement was downplayed; when the expedition returned home, it was virtually ignored. Finch and Bruce had climbed to 27,300 feet using oxygen, whereas Mallory, Norton, and Somervell attained 26,985 feet and less horizontal distance toward the summit. Yet it was the oxygenless effort that reaped most of the attention and praise.

The Mount Everest Committee remained equivocal: Without having any real faith in the equipment nor a consensus that it should be used, the committee decided to supply it to the next expedition in 1924. The 1922 system had been adapted from the standard apparatus used by the Royal Air Force. Some slight modifications were made to the design between 1922 and 1924, and larger capacity oxygen bottles were employed on the latter expedition, allowing three cylinders to carry the same amount of gas as four of the old style. But the weight remained much the same—from 32-33 pounds—until modified by Irvine. In both years there were serious leakages from the cylinders during the course of the expeditions.

In 1953, when Everest was climbed by a British party, the oxygen-breathing equipment used was simpler and more reliable, largely as a result of engineering advances made during the Second World War. But of course it also drew on the experience of the pioneering Everest expeditions. With better cylinders holding gas at higher pressure, it was possible to provide a climber with up to six liters of oxygen per minute, as opposed to the two-liter maximum delivered in the 1920s. It was not until 1978 that the summit of Everest was reached without the use of any supplemental oxygen at all by the Tyrolean climbers Reinhold Messner and Peter Habeler. Many climbers have now been to the top without relying on supplemental oxygen, some of them many times (Ang Rita has climbed Everest a remarkable ten times without oxygen). But by far the majority prefer to take advantage of oxygen's beneficent help and to enjoy the experience.

OXYGEN DUMP ON THE NORTH COL, 1922

GEOFFREY BRUCE TESTING APPARATUS NEAR ADVANCE BASE CAMP, 1922

were prepared to sit it out with him, rather than give up the attempt. Around six that evening they heard voices outside and were delighted to see Sherpas who brought up thermoses of hot tea and Bovril from the Col. That evening they breathed some of their oxygen to bring life back to frozen extremities, and at night rigged up a device that gave them each a small, continuous supply to ensure some sleep. Before daybreak on the 27th they were thawing out boots over a candle and, as the first sunshine caught the tent, they were away.

Tejbir, lacking wind-proof clothing, began to flag. At 26,000 feet he collapsed. Sharing out his load between them, they sent him back to wait in the tent. Soon after, Finch decided to strike out across the North Face rather than continue toward the Shoulder. It meant tackling the slabby ledges, again under a covering of loose new snow, but it would be out of the worst of the wind. Bruce seemed sure-footed enough, and they climbed unroped for speed, sticking close together. The ground steepened, in some places treacherously, but Bruce kept up well. In places, they stopped to change cylinders, sending the empty ones clanging down the hillside while shouting, "Another 5 lbs off our backs!"

Their horizontal progress was good, but they were not ascending. Finch opted for a more diagonal line, and the next time they looked at their barometer it read 27,300 feet,

George Finch and Geoffrey Bruce used oxygen during their 1922 attempt to reach the summit. Roped together at 23,000 feet on the North Col, Finch photographed Bruce crossing a crevasse. The peak in the background is Khartaphu.

higher than all the other peaks around, except the summit pyramid that beckoned ahead. Then, Bruce let out a startled cry. His oxygen was no longer flowing and he was stumbling dangerously. Finch moved swiftly. Grabbing him by the shoulder—just as he was about to topple backward—he guided him onto a ledge, then handed him his own oxygen while he fixed up a T-piece to enable them both to breathe from the same set while the faulty connection in Bruce's was replaced.

Finch could see that, like Tejbir, Bruce had driven himself to the limit: If they went on, even a few thousand feet more, it was almost certain they would not both get back alive. Until then the prospect of failure had not occurred to him—"the summit was there before us; a little longer, and we should be on the top." In just a moment, that vision vanished. They roped up and retreated.

Tramping down, they could hear their porters coming up to meet them. Telling Tejbir to return with the porters, they continued on to the broken snows of the North Col, arriving there "deplorably tired" at 4 p.m. Captain Noel was in residence, having spent three nights there, and after a snack of tea and spaghetti they continued down with his help. They reached Camp III at 5:30 p.m., 40 minutes after leaving the col. They had descended over 6,000 feet since midday and were, as Finch remarked, "quite finished."

By rights this is where the story of 1922 should have ended and, if Longstaff had had his way, it would have. The height record had been broken not once, but twice, though in the process almost all were hors de combat, in one way or another. Geoffrey Bruce's feet and Morshead's hands were so badly frostbitten they were definitely out of the reckoning. Norton, too, could not walk. Mallory had a frostbitten finger, and his heart was exhibiting a worrying "thrill." Finch was exhausted and his heart enlarged. Somervell alone presented no symptoms of any significance. But Longstaff was not the only doctor, and second opinions were solicited from Somervell and Wakefield whose diagnoses were not so gloomy. Should they not build on the valuable experience gained, and make one last all-out bid for the summit?

Finch and Bruce had not only climbed 215 vertical feet higher than Mallory's party, they had gained an extra horizontal mile on the summit. It was enough to convert Mallory to the oxygen camp. He would use it. He slipped off to write to Ruth, telling her, "Dear love, believe that I will never forget the beautiful way you have behaved about this adventure." It is another of his letters of conscience, making peace with her when he knows that what he is about to do carries great risk. As much, he admits to David Pye, telling him it is "an infernal mountain, cold and treacherous. Frankly the game is not good enough: the risks of getting caught are too great; the margin of

Finch and Bruce were photographed by Wakefield as they headed back into Camp IV at 23,000 feet. Their failed summit attempt proved, to some, the value of oxygen at high altitude. Finch (at rear) wears his prototype down suit; fellow climbers made fun of it, but the suit kept him warmer than the others.

Porters (above) descend from the North Col. Bruce, frostbitten and exhausted, was assisted into Camp III by a Sherpa (opposite), followed by expedition cinematographer Noel and two Sherpas, one carrying Finch's skis. The climbers were, in Finch's words, "Dead, dead, beat."

strength when men are at great heights is too small. Perhaps it's mere folly to go up again. But how can I be out of the hunt?"

So it happened that while Longstaff, Strutt, and Finch escorted Morshead down to India for medical treatment, most of the others tramped back up. On June 7, Somervell, Mallory, and Crawford were leading 14 porters up the snow-heavy flanks of the North Col when an avalanche caught the whole party. There were four ropes of men, the sahibs all on the first rope, scouting the way. They were about half way. Mallory was coming up last on his rope when at about 1:30 p.m. he heard a noise "not unlike an explosion of untamped gunpowder." Although he had never experienced an avalanche, he knew immediately what was coming. A relatively small snowslab had broken away a few yards to their right and was sliding toward them. Those on his rope were only lightly covered and quickly extricated themselves; those of the group immediately behind them were deposited a hundred feet lower down. Of the remaining nine men, there was no sign. They had been carried over an ice cliff of more than 40 feet. The crevasse below was filled with avalanched snow. The fall alone had killed most of them. Two men were

rescued alive with no severe injures, but everyone else was dead.

Noel and Wakefield, back in III, knew at once something had happened. They had been watching through glasses as the party wound up the steep wall, but glanced away momentarily. "When I looked back the whole wall was white," Wakefield wrote in his diary. The string of men had gone. At first he thought they had all been wiped off by the avalanche, but as the fuzz cleared he could make out some figures still on the slope. At once he and Noel made up a relief party and hurried up to help. Noel himself had narrowly escaped being among them. He had been last in the line of climbers, but found the going too heavy with all his photographic equipment, and had turned back. The seven fatalities were all those at the end of the column.

Mallory and Somervell were devastated. "Why, oh why could not one of us Britishers have shared their fate?" Somervell railed. Mallory felt the burden of blame, though sought in letters to reassure Younghusband, Young, Strutt, and other Alpine friends that it was not the result of recklessness on their part. Privately, the general was not so sure. To Strutt, he confided, "I do not believe personally, if Finch had been a fit man, it could have occurred....I begged them before they left to exert the very greatest care, and there wasn't the least necessity to risk mens' lives, let alone their own, to recover a few tents from the North Col."

Everest had rebuffed the expedition's best efforts by the time this picture was taken of the oxygen-free team (from left: Morshead, Mallory, Somervell, and Norton). Nevertheless, the party returned to Base Camp having established a new altitude record.

ENROUTE TO INDIA ON THE RMS CALIFORNIA, MALLORY AND HIS CLIMBING PARTNER ANDREW "SANDY" IRVINE SAIL TOWARD DESTINY.

CHAPTER FOUR

What you need to get up Everest is P.B.S.—pure bloody sweat.

T. G. LONGSTAFF, 1922

ROUND ONE

Many friends of George Mallory would later testify that he became "possessed" by Everest. John Noel used to say he was absolutely obsessed with getting to the top, that the mountain had a "mental grip" on him. Geoffrey Keynes thought his reported response on being asked why he wanted to climb this mountain—"Because it's there"—if true, betrayed "pyschological fixation." And this was reinforced in Keynes' mind when George told him before his last and fatal trip to Everest that what he faced would be more like war than adventure, and that he doubted he would return alive.

We cannot know how much these reminiscences are colored by the way events played out. Certainly, after 1922, there could be no false sense of adventure. The blithe optimism of earlier efforts had of necessity been replaced with stern realism. No longer were they investigating the unknown: They knew exactly what they were up against. And, after the tragic avalanche, they'd had a taste of the perils involved. Until then, it was almost as if expedition members led a charmed existence on this mountain, surviving from one miracle to another. The slip coming down after the first climbing attempt could so easily have resulted in the deaths of four men, as they were plucked one after the other from the slope. Only Mallory's prompt and instinctive ice-ax belay held them—an action taken after eight or nine hours of strenuous activity on the hill. Fumbling among the seracs on the North Col in the dark, without lantern or torch, could equally have spelled disaster—as Finch and Bruce, too, came within a hair of toppling into oblivion when Bruce's oxygen set failed. The awareness that they were on borrowed time was growing all the time. Yet George Mallory had a strong sense of duty: To himself and his family, yes, he knew his obligations; but at the same time he was a child of Empire and conscious of what England expected. He could not then (or ever) accept that he had given enough. Of the decision to make that third, and ultimately disastrous, attempt in 1922, against all odds and despite his own intuition that it was mere foolishness now the snow had come, he'd said, "It was too early to turn back, and too easy—we should not have been satisfied afterwards."

Mallory blamed himself for the loss of the porters. Perhaps more than anyone other than the general, he had worried over their welfare, and deplored the cavalier way unroped men had been left by Finch to find their own way up and down sections of mountain. The irony that despite his good intentions, it was he who was responsible for their return to that fatal slope was almost too great to bear. "I'm too much grieved for personal reminiscences," he wrote to his father. "But such things can't easily be put aside, nor I feel ought they to be. What is done can't be undone...and the worst of this case is that nothing can be done to make good." And to Ruth he wrote, "The consequences of my mistake are so terrible; it seems impossible to believe that it has happend for ever and that I can do nothing to make good. There is no obligation I have so much wanted to honour as that of taking care of those men."

This burden of guilt oppressed him for months, but there was no way he could put Everest aside. He and Finch were committed to a series of lectures to satisfy public curiousity and refill the coffers of the Mount Everest Committee. By now, the quest to put a man on top of the world had taken on a momentum of its own. Undoubtedly, there would be other attempts; everyone expected it. The only decision to be made was how soon the next one could take place.

First, conclusions needed to be drawn from the experience gained in 1922. Beyond appreciating the real nature of the difficulties ahead, what else did they know? On the plus side, as George told the Joint Meeting of the Royal Geographical Society and the Alpine Club, were the porters. Their strength and support were far greater than had been expected. Loads were carried as high as 25,000 feet, and some individuals even repeated this achievement on three successive days, exhibiting astonishingly little fatigue. It convinced him that a sixth camp

A novice skier on the slopes of Mürren, Switzerland, Irvine (right) was a less than accomplished mountain climber. He was a surprise selection for the team, and was given the unglamorous post of equipment officer. But as the 1924 Everest Expedition members gathered for a publicity photograph in Darjeeling (below), Irvine and Mallory were already seated together at the center of the portrait (Mallory in hat).

Relaxing in the Sikkim forest enroute to Everest, Irvine napped by a mountain stream.

could almost certainly be carried to around 27,000 feet, so that "the limit of climbing, instead of being determined by the difficulty of fixing camps, will be determined simply by the factor of endurance among the trained climbers." Mallory did not think the prospect of a party climbing the last 2,000 feet to the summit in a day was in itself fantastic, but their own experience with wind and weather in 1922 did little to raise hopes. Without longer respite, chances of reaching it and getting down in safety were all too small. "Man may calculate how to solve his problem, and...you may finish the sentence," he ended enigmatically.

This lecture, the first of the new round for him and Finch, was delivered on October 16, 1922, at the Central Hall, Westminster. Both men were lively performers and to promote their program much was made in the press of their differences of approach. Mallory was still equivocal toward oxygen use. Its assistance was beneficial, he accepted, but he could not bring himself to believe that the final feet of Everest were absolutely unclimbable without it. And he had delighted his audience by saying he'd told one learned physiologist, "Experiments made in a pumped-out tank, interesting as they may be, are of no value in determining where precisely on that hill of unrivalled altitude persevering man will be brought to a standstill." His message for the scientists was that they might "explode themselves in their diabolical chamber, but we would do what we could to explode their damnable heresy!" Said in half-jest for effect, it nonetheless fanned the differences between himself and Finch.

Hinks would have liked to see an advance party back in Tibet by the end of the year, to set up a permanent base camp that could relieve future expeditions of the preliminary chore of building a supply line; climbers could then follow as early as January, training in the Alps on the way, perhaps, so as to be poised and fit from the start of the season. This was impractical. More time was needed to work on the design of the oxygen apparatus, as it was for fund-raising. The lecture tours were not proving as lucrative as was hoped, nor indeed was Captain Noel's cine film, largely due to a mix-up in selling foreign rights. For one reason or another—which included the failure of the Alliance Bank in Simla that crashed taking £700 of the committee's money with it—a further effort was deferred until 1924.

In early 1923 Mallory undertook his North American lecture tour, which, though it kept him and Ruth apart once more, was for the most part entertaining. He started out in New York where he was installed in the Waldorf Astoria, enjoying the novelty of being a "swell"—Prohibition, or no. He caught up with old friends, made new ones, and looked up distant relations. He was coming to love his lecturing—and he would write excitedly to Ruth whenever he had a particularly responsive audience. His speaking voice was good, and he had a relaxed stage manner. There was no doubt his Everest experiences had matured him, and brought him confidence. Friends remarked on a new serenity about him; the old impatience was gone. David Pye felt that "the perfect equability which he had always shown as a climber had taken a deeper hold, so that his charm of appearance and temperament became no longer a separate quality, but the inevitable expression of the whole man." The fire was still there, and all the old idealism, but allied to tolerance and sympathy. George wondered if his new communications skills could ever be related to "anything more useful in the future."

He was abroad for three months, though not enough venues had been arranged for it to be a truly profitable enterprise. Proceeds, after the agent's expenses, were shared between the committee and himself; one lecture in Montreal made only $48. "What a washout!" he lamented to Ruth. "We shall be poorer than I hoped for a bit." Yet, he saw little prospect of changing the situation; what could he do but more lecturing on behalf of the Everest Committee? "And there goes the spring I had hoped to be spending at home"—He wondered if he had been right to give up schoolmastering. He, Geoffrey Young, and David Pye had long planned to set up a revolutionary new type of school, but the idea was no nearer to fruition. And here, fate and friends took a hand. Soon after his return, the opportunity of a position arose with the Board of Extra-Mural Studies in Cambridge. It was Hinks who heard of it and put his name forward, while Benson and other friends rallied round with references. Against quite strong opposition, Mallory landed the job and threw himself enthusiastically into his new life as assistant secretary and lecturer to the Board, organising tutorial classes for working men and women. His Fabian instincts were well satisfied. For the moment, he put from his mind any thought of going to Everest again, and made plans to move Ruth and the children from Godalming to Cambridge.

"We started from Pedong this morning," George wrote to Ruth from Rongli on March 29, 1924. "—sloped easily down the 2,000 feet to the stream...there Irvine, Odell, and I bathed, properly this time, even finding a pool to dive into."

By mid-year a screening committee was formed to build the team to go to Everest in 1924. Under General Bruce's leadership, it was hoped to include some new blood around a nucleus of old hands. The indefatigable Somervell; Teddy Norton (who Bruce described as "the great success" of 1922 and nominated as his second in command); Geoffrey Bruce (as a climber rather than a transport officer); and Mallory, if he were free to come—these were obvious choices. But what of Finch? The committee was divided. It was true Finch had demonstrated that, given good weather, Everest could almost certainly be climbed with oxygen; but the degree to which a climber had been shown to acclimatize—that too was encouraging. While not climbing quite as high as Finch, Mallory's party had not fallen far short. It appeared almost as convincing that an oxygenless party could succeed in the right circumstances. There was still strong antipathy for the clumsy apparatus and, by extension, for its chief advocate. Younghusband was not alone in thinking it

ROUTES OF THE 1921, 1922, AND 1924 MOUNT EVEREST EXPEDITIONS

Irvine demonstrates the "Roarer Cooker" to wary Sherpa cooks during the Tibetan portion of their Everest trek.

The map (left), shows the Mount Everest region topography, as we know it today. Names reflect features as they were known in the 1920s.

a tragedy that such a magnificent mountaineer as Finch, with his experience and skill, should have been "led astray" by science when he might have been the very man to have got up without oxygen. After dithering for months whether or not to include him on the team, at the last minute Finch's name was dropped.

The newcomers would include Noel Odell, a geologist with plenty of Alpine experience, and Bentley Beetham, schoolmaster and regular climbing partner of Somervell. John de Vars Hazard was also signed up—an engineer and close friend and wartime colleague of Morshead, he had served in India as a sapper. E.C. Shebbeare of the Indian Forest Service would be transport officer, and Maj. R. W. G. Hingston, the medical officer.

And then there was Andrew Irvine. It had long been felt that the Everest parties needed some younger men. Irvine, known to everyone as "Sandy," was an engineering student known to both Odell and Longstaff from an Oxford University expedition to Spitsbergen the previous year, when he had shown himself to be an ideal companion on a rugged exercise: physically strong, resourceful and perpetually cheerful. He had next to no climbing experience and, at 21, was younger than had been envisaged; but he was known to be a mechanical genius, and it was this talent that tipped the balance. In the absence of Finch, Odell had been appointed "Oxygen Officer," but he was abroad prior to the expedition's departure, and Irvine set himself to find out as much about the apparatus as he could. No one yet knew whether someone of Irvine's age would acclimatize as well as an older man. General Bruce introduced him in an early press release as the expedition's "experiment," and Mallory wrote to Geoffrey Young, "Irvine represents our attempt to get one superman, though lack of experience is against him."

Mallory could put off his decision no longer. "I'm having a horrible time on the tightrope," he wrote to Hinks. "I suppose it is certain that Bruce feels as strongly as you put it? It might make a difference...." He half hoped the Board would say that he could not be spared from his new duties so that he would not be obliged to choose between two forces. "It will be a big sacrifice for me either way," he told Ruth. "You must tell me if you can't bear the idea of me going again, and that will settle it anyway."

There was no resistance from his Cambridge Board, and Ruth knew him well enough to know how grim he would find it to see others, without him, engaged in the battle for the summit. She could not insist he stay. Geoffrey Young alone vainly urged him to pass up the opportunity, but by then the die was cast. Mallory told his father, "My present feeling is that I have to look at it from the point of view of loyalty to the expedition and of carrying through a task begun."

On February 29, 1924, Mallory joined Irvine, Beetham and Hazard aboard the R.M.S. *California* for the journey to India. If there had been any reluctance on his part, he put it behind him and threw himself into the now familiar role of Everest campaigner.

Mallory and Irvine hit it off from the beginning. On the boat Mallory wrote home to say he found the young man "sensible and not at all highly strung. He looked just the sort of person to depend upon for anything—except perhaps conversation." Mallory was already putting his mind to tactics and considering possible pairings on the mountain. If his, as he now expected, was to be an attempt with oxygen—the matter after all had to be finished this year; merely another height record would not be enough—then it would make sense for him to partner Odell or Irvine, who knew most about the equipment. Yet it was Irvine who was proving the ablest at managing the temperamental apparatus. In his mind George was already incorporating Irvine into his plans, without ever having climbed with him. From the boat, he wrote to his sister Mary, "Irvine is a great dab at things mechanical and has some criticisms to make; and there are certainly a good many chances that it [the oxygen] will go wrong or break if we use it.... However, I rather expect we shall use it, as we can carry 50 per cent more oxygen than last year with the same weight.... We've got to get up this time; and if we wait for it and make full preparations, instead of dashing up at the first moment, some of us will reach the summit, I believe.... I wish Irvine had had a season in the Alps."

By the time the company reached Shegar Dzong, equipment manager Irvine had designed a major modification for the oxygen tanks. He inverted them, placing the valves at the bottom for more reliable operation. Irvine called it the Mark-V version.

Mary and her husband now lived in Colombo, in what was then Ceylon. The annual monsoon was known to hit Ceylon some three weeks before it reached the Himalaya. After discussions with Norton, it suddenly occurred to Mallory to ask his sister to send

him postcards every five days or so to say what the weather was doing with her, and a telegram when it was certain that the monsoon had started. To aid Noel's film outfit, a better and faster system of mail-runners had been organised this time. Mary's forecasts, it was hoped, could arrive in time to influence the timing of the last climbing efforts of the season.

It was a happy, optimistic party that had gathered in Darjeeling. Bruce was in fine fettle, though there had been some concern over his blood pressure this year. He was asked to submit himself to a further medical examination in Darjeeling. He did not—postponing that until they were at Yatung in Tibet, where Hingston was persuaded to let him proceed. Norton had put a tremendous amount of thought and effort into both the equipment and its transport and organization. Mallory was impressed, declaring him an ideal second to Bruce. He was delighted, too, to see Somervell again, who since the last expedition had given up the opportunity of a lucrative London job for the life of a mission doctor in South India. Odell, who joined the party from the Persian oil fields, appeared "one of the best." He told Ruth, "Really it is an amazingly nice party."

Irvine, too, was enjoying the exotic shock of India, its people and sights. He started a diary, and he made a point in Darjeeling of looking up Lady Lytton, wife of the Governer of Bengal and mother of his friend Tony Knebsworth, with whom he had been skiing earlier in the year. The second entry in his diary records: "Spent afternoon playing tennis with the Lyttons, with the result that I have only just finished my packing (1 a.m., March 24)." He had been appointed "Mess Secretary," which involved keeping an eye on, and knowing how to work the various items of apparatus—including the new paraffin Roarer Cookers, which were like enormous brazing lamps.

The journey through Sikkim was delightful with magnolias and rhododendrons at their peak. Below Pedong, Mallory, Odell, and Irvine raced down the 2,000 feet to Rongpo Chu bridge, where Noel had immortalized Mallory taking a splash in 1922—a decorous sort of bath destined for public consumption. This time with no cine cameras in sight, and just the three of them, Mallory was able, as he told Ruth, to bathe "properly" and at length, even finding a pool to dive into. Irvine records another dip later in the day at Rongli, where the water was not so deep. "Spent most of the afternoon rolling on hot rocks or in the stream floating over rapids and small waterfalls," he wrote. "Did this once too often and scratched my bottom rather." There were more people about this time, and he was taken to one side and told it would be better to wear "drawers" in future, as the locals and porters thought it quite wrong for a Sahib, or even one of themselves, to expose themselves in a state of nudity.

Despite the diversions of the trail, at the end of the day Mallory's thoughts winged home

As if waving a warning flag, Everest spreads its white mist pennant against the horizon as Mallory and Irvine, in brimmed hats, rest with their porters on Pang La pass. It was from here that Mallory first sighted Everest in 1921—and where 74 years later Mallory's son John gazed at the mountain that immortalized his father.

to Ruth, as they usually did. "Dear girl," he wrote, "I think of you often and often and with ever so much love and wish for your company. Would there were some way of bringing you nearer. I think the nearness depends very much upon the state of one's imagination. When it boils up, as it does sometimes, at night under the stars, I could whisper in your ear; and even now dear I do feel near you, though my state is loggish, and I come very near to kissing you...."

At Yatung, where Hingston gave Bruce the OK to continue, there were already signs that the general was not as fit as could be hoped. Irvine's diary, written on the day of the "medical," noted that Bruce was having a rest day because he felt "a little bit seedy." And, though he told some good stories at dinner the next night, Somervell remarked how feverish he was, not at all fit. At Phari, three days later, the general celebrated his 58th birthday with a bottle of 140-year-old rum, but feeling fragile the next morning opted for the lower, Kellas route around to Kampa Dzong. Hingston and John MacDonald (son of the Trade Officer and in charge of getting Noel's photographs back for *The Times*) would accompany him on this lengthier detour. Mallory wrote in confidence to Ruth: "The General's trouble has been an

Norton's watercolor of Cho Uyo (right) depicts the view from Pang La during the 1922 approach march.

irregular pulse and he and Hingston are both nervous about the state of his heart." And with good reason, remembering what happened to the younger Kellas on this same stretch of route. "It is difficult to know how much to make of this trouble," Mallory added, telling Ruth not to mention it. "I think it is 10 to 1 he will be all right."

Over the next few days word came that the general had come down with malaria and nearly died in Tuna. He'd had to be carried back to Yatung on a litter. Hingston was sufficiently alarmed to escort him back into Sikkim and would not hear of him rejoining the expedition. He informed the Mount Everest Committee that Bruce's trouble was solely "the recrudescence of old malarial infection...rendered active the cold and wind of Tibet." The general's heart had remained sound, but he'd lost two stones in weight and his spleen was dangerously enlarged. "I insist relinquishment," he cabled. "Await report." This was a blow and opinions among committee members were split over what to do if the general took matters into his own hands and tried to come back. The veteran Norman Collie remarked that Bruce was old enough to look after himself. "If every explorer who had fever were to turn back," he said, "a great deal of exploration would never be done."

Bruce submitted without struggle, however, and on April 19 Norton took over as expedition leader, appointing Mallory his second-in-command and leader of the climbing party. "We shall miss him [Bruce] a great deal in the mess as you may imagine," Mallory wrote to Younghusband, "and we shall miss his moral force behind the porters later on." But, in the same letter, he wanted to reassure those at home that the enterprise would not suffer: "I must tell you, what Norton can't say in a dispatch, that we have a splendid leader in him. He knows the whole *bandobast* from A to Z, and his eyes are everywhere; is personally acceptable to everyone and makes us all feel happy, as always full of interest, easy and yet dignified, or rather never losing dignity, and a tremendous adventurer—he's dead keen to have a dash with the non-oxygen party. He tells me (and I tell you confidentially, as I'm sure he wouldn't have it broadcast) that when the time comes he must leave it to me in consultation with Somervell to decide whether he'll be the right man for the job. Isn't that the right spirit to bring to Mount Everest."

The long journey across Tibet was enlivened with endless discussions aimed at preparing a plan of campaign. By the time Shegar was reached, two weeks before getting to base camp, Norton was satisfied enough to have had a table typed up detailing the exact daily program of porters' and climbers' moves. It had weaknesses, not least in its complication. And it depended on almost half their porters being able to carry to 25,500 ft or higher, and some to go to at least 27,000 feet. Base camp was to be reached on April 29, and four climbers were to be ready to begin the upward trek within four days. "On May 17, or thereabouts," George told Ruth, "we should reach the summit. I'm eager for the

great events to begin." This time, Norton was determined there should be no fatalities and no time wasted.

Rongbuk greeted them with "the most unpleasant weather"—snow and a bitterly cold wind—yet on their first day in camp they were able to send 150 loaded Tibetan porters up toward the site for Camp II on the East Rongbuk glacier. The role of shepherding these men and establishing the first two glacier camps was put in the hands of the expedition's three Gurkha non-commissioned officers, two of whom had climbed with the previous expedition. Mallory was responsible for provisioning the upper camps. He and Norton had another long powwow, going over the intricacies of their agreed plan, aimed at getting two groups of two to the top more or less together, one with, one without oxygen.

Keeping track of what each porter carried over this period, when and to where, would be tricky, he told Ruth, but was necessary to monitor the mens' acclimatization and fitness. And carries would need to get started up onto the col as well, while the lower camps were being equipped. He hoped Beetham and Hazard could set up Camp IV, while he and Irvine had "a canter up to about 23,000," up the east ridge of Changtse, partly to get a better look at camping sites on the mountain and partly to have a trial run. It would give him some idea

Faces set with determination, the 1924 expedition team posed for the camera at Base Camp: From left (rear): Irvine, Mallory, Norton, Odell, and John Macdonald (a Times *runner); (front): Shebbeare, Geoffrey Bruce, Somervell, and Beetham.*

what to expect from Irvine, although he had no doubts on that score. As he wrote to his sister Mary, Irvine was both a mechanical genius and a tower of strength, "an absolutely sound fellow right through, and he'll go well on the mountain and make no rash or silly steps. I somehow feel we are going to get there this time." But whether they made it or not, he reassured her, it would be his job to get the party off the mountain in safety. "And I'm keen about that part too—no one climber or porter is going to get killed if I can help it—that would spoil all."

Yet there were no two ways about it: This was a highly optimistic program—even if everyone had been fit. But Beetham had not been up to par since contracting dysentery in Sikkim. He'd only narrowly escaped being sent back and, though recovering slowly, he was a long way from the bubbly old Beetham, once described as "the kind of man that nothing less than a ton of bricks could keep down: nineteen hundredweight would have been of no use." And Hazard, too, was an unknown quantity. He had a good record of climbing in Britain and the Alps, had made some good rock routes in the Lake District with such pioneers as F. Botterill and E. E. Roberts, but he had kept to himself on this trip, and had "built a psychological wall round himself," as Somervell described it.

On cue, four climbers left base on May 3, Odell replacing Beetham. They were expecting to be away for a fortnight, and Irvine had packed an emergency toolbox that he hoped would cope with all contingencies. Before setting out, all four had blood samples taken by Somervell for a hemaglobin test. Irvine noted proudly that he

Heavily weighed down with equipment and supplies, porters prepare to depart Base Camp.

could boast the greatest percentage of red corpuscles, Odell coming second. The day was cold and threatening ("mildly bloody" in Irvine's opinion), and the porters soon lagged behind. Most had brought blankets and other gear in addition to their loads and were struggling under the weight. The plan had been to have *sangars* ready for their arrival at Camp II the next day, rock walls that could be roofed with a tent fly, but no work had started on these yet, even though the NCO-in-charge was in residence, with two assistants. Seeing that 23 men urgently needed housing, Mallory and Irvine fell to wall-building as soon as they arrived. Before long some of the porters joined in. "It is an extraordinary thing to watch the conversion of men from listlessness to some spirit of enterprise," wrote Mallory to Ruth. Soon they were singing as they worked. But two-and-a-half hours of boulder-shifting brought a nosebleed for Irvine, and he took a deserved rest, while Mallory and Odell scouted the onward route to Camp III.

The weather was no better on the 5th, with snow blowing off the glacier, but the plan held: Break trail and get stores up to Camp III. All four Sahibs accompanied the protesting porters along the glassy trough between the ice seracs, exhorting, driving, pushing. At least here it was sheltered, but as they came out onto the open glacier, a vicious wind blew straight off the North Col. Everyone was feeling the altitude, and it was 6 o'clock in the evening, with the sun already

gone from the basin, when they reached the site for the camp and quickly pitched a few tents. No soup could be found among the loads, and much of the food they could find was frozen. After a spartan meal they turned in for a cold night.

Irvine was surprised to see Mallory up at 6:30 the next morning, ready to go down and sort out the stores situation. "Energetic bugger," he thought to himself, as he rolled over in his bag for another couple hours of sleep before breakfast (which proved to be a sausage and half a tin of condensed milk). It was a lost sort of day, trying to improve conditions all round. Mallory was worried that the heart might go out of the porters. Those laboring up from Camp II to Camp III he had dump their loads about three-quarters of the way, and turn back. As things were, he didn't feel Camp III could accommodate more at the moment. Irvine and Odell came down to the dump to round up more stoves and other vital items.

The morning of the 7th was even worse. The night temperature had fallen to minus 21°F. All the porters were sick, many of them vomiting, and some in a very bad way. Mallory had to physically haul them from their tents. One poor man had feet so dangerously swollen from the cold that his boots could only be pulled on without socks, and he couldn't walk without support. It was clear that they had to go down quickly. Mallory escorted the sorry party toward Camp II, before handing them over to the care of one of the NCOs; he then assisted the few stalwarts coming up to Camp III. Odell

FILMING ON EVEREST

"The ever-present Noel" is what his companions called Capt. John Noel on the Everest expeditions of 1922 and 1924. He was the official photographer and filmmaker to both ventures. At a time when motion pictures were still in their infancy, he took his specially adapted Newton-Sinclair 35mm camera to 23,000 feet on the North Col to immortalize the efforts of the climbers. He used to boast that from a camera position he had set up in rocks on one of the eastern buttresses of Changtse, above Advance Base Camp, he could see every step of the north side route, all the way to the summit. From here, his "Eagle's Nest" at 22,000 feet, the pyramid of Everest was some three miles away in a straight line. On summit attempts, he would keep his 20-inch telephoto lens trained on the pyramid while scanning the summit area with his "finder telescope" for microscopic figures.

Noel admired the work of the fine mountain photographer Vittorio Sella, but his great hero was Herbert Ponting, who had accompanied Robert Scott's expedition to the Antarctic in 1910-11. Noel used to say that he'd seen Ponting's film of Scott's last expedition at least 16 times and he considered it the most successful documentary ever made.

CAPT. JOHN NOEL WITH HIS NEWTON-SINCLAIR ON THE NORTH COL, 1922

Following his father into the army, Noel chose a regiment in north India, and every summer, when his garrison retired from the heat of the plains into the hills, he would spend his vacation wandering the border country of Sikkim, looking for ways into forbidden Tibet. His objective was to approach Mount Everest; at the time no Westerner had been within 40 or 50 miles of it. In 1913, with a small band of hillsmen, he crossed an unguarded pass north of Kangchenjunga and came within 40 miles of the great mountain before being turned back by Tibetan soldiers. His lecture of his adventures to the Royal Geographical Society, given after the First World War, was instrumental in launching the Everest expeditions of the 1920s.

The War Office could not be persuaded to give Noel sufficient leave to take part in the 1921 reconnaissance, but he resigned his commission and made sure he was available as the official photographer for the climbing attempt planned in 1922. The Everest Committee, which organized these expeditions, was very conservative, and many of its members, including its influential secretary, Arthur Hinks, had a deep aversion to publicity. There was never any question of taking along an ordinary professional filmmaker, lest he "vulgarize" the effort. Nor was the idea of a film immediately popular with the climbers: "I didn't come to Everest to become a film star," the photogenic George Mallory told Noel. All the same, after sharing a tent with the photographer at Base Camp, Mallory became intrigued with the whole process and would help Noel in his developing tent.

Noel's previous filmmaking had included some instructional films for the School of Musketry at Hythe, and a documentary about the caviar industry in the Caspian Sea. He and Hinks put their heads together before 1922 to come up with an ideal photographic outfit. Besides the still cameras, he would take three cinematograph cameras. His favorite was the Newton-Sinclair. Modeled on the camera used by Ponting in the Antarctic, it was constructed of duralumin for lightness and had special point bearings requiring no oil at all, as this had a tendency to freeze in low temperatures. Ponting had told Noel that at times his tongue froze to his camera. With this in mind, Noel asked Mr. Newman, the designer, to make a rubber camera cover, so he could press his face against it to steady it in a high wind without fear of his cheeks cleaving to the cold metal. Fully loaded, with 400 feet of film, the camera weighed less than 20 pounds—just over half the weight of the IMAX camera used by David Breashears on Everest in 1996.

Noel's maxim was that "development should always be carried out in the field, within 14 days of exposure." Apart from anything else, this gave him an indication of what he was getting. Accordingly, in 1922 he supplied himself with a special light-proof photographic tent and developing tanks, in which—at Base Camp—he developed, fixed, and washed thousands of feet of 35mm film—hanging it to dry over a yak-dung stove. When the expedition left for home and he still had film in need of processing, he removed the whole process to Gyantse, where he set up a darkroom in the town's old fort. He returned home with his film in time for its first screening at the Central Hall, Westminster.

Unfortunately, the November night of the showing was plagued by one of London's infamous

CAPT. NOEL'S LIGHT-PROOF TENT USED FOR DEVELOPING FILM AT BASE CAMP

CAPTAIN NOEL'S "EAGLE'S NEST" VANTAGE POINT AT 22,000 FEET

"pea-soupers," and the large auditorium filled with fog. That and the lack of music (added later) made the film's debut rather less spectacular than later showings. *Climbing Mount Everest* subsequently enjoyed a 10-week run at the Philharmonic Hall, where it proved a sellout—even if George Bernard Shaw thought the expedition resembled nothing so much as "a picnic in Connemara surprised by a snowstorm."

The film's strength lay in the travel scenes and landscape shots and in its depiction of life on the Tibetan Plateau. There were fine sequences of "devil dancing" by the monks of the Rongbuk Monastery, from whom Howard Somervell had collected Tibetan folk music. The mountaineering section recorded the expedition's passage through the ice seracs of the East Rongbuk Glacier to the reluctant withdrawal after the avalanche tragedy. Especially praised were Noel's studies of "rushing cloud and wind-swept snow" captured on panchromatic film with the help of red and yellow filters. From the North Col he photographed Finch's oxygen attempt until the party was lost among the dark rocks at somewhere above 25,000 feet. He had hoped there might be a still photograph at least to illustrate the highest point gained, but Finch—who dedicatedly took over 2,000 photographs during the journey and expedition—had been too exercised with managing the oxygen apparatus to have the time or inclination for photography above the North Col. Noel had held back from "intimate" shots for fear of annoying the climbers; and besides, as he said, they could be rather quarrelsome—Mallory once said that each expedition started out as one party of twelve and returned twelve parties of one.

One of the many difficulties in photographing at extreme altitudes had proved to be the effect of the dry Tibetan climate on Cine-film, which cracks and sparkles with electric static when pulled through the hand; it was necessary to work with a wet hand when threading the film on the developing frames. The problem had been anticipated, and Newman-Sinclair was successful in making the film run through the gate without friction. He had also designed open-mouthed magazines to minimize the damage. The sheer effort of fighting lethargy to film at altitude was perhaps the hardest part. "You have to fight against yourself," Noel said in a later interview. "Your fingers fumble with a screw, and you drop the screw. You just don't care."

Noel was sufficiently encouraged by the film's success that he put an extraordinary proposition to the Everest Committee. He offered to purchase the entire film and photographic rights to the 1924 expedition for the impressive sum of £8,000—to be paid in advance of departure. At a stroke, this removed all financial burdens from the committee, and the offer was accepted gladly. Noel was responsible for providing all his own equipment, film stock, transportation to Tibet, and whatever porters and photographic assistants he required. In return, banking on the likelihood of success this time, he was looking for an adventure film with sufficient public interest to break into the main cinema circuits of the world. It was an attractive proposition, and his shareholders included Sir Francis Younghusband and the Aga Khan. This time he would not do his own developing. Instead, he had a custom-made "laboratory" built in the corner of a friend's garden in Darjeeling. All exposed film was rushed there by relays of special runners and horsemen. Two photographic assistants, Pereira and King, worked full-time to process all film and photographs, supplying newspapers and Pathé News with regular pictures. A number of improvements had been made to the camera equipment: Arthur Newman fitted an electric motor to Noel's camera, geared to permit time-lapse photography, a novel feature in those days; and the long telephoto lens was given steadying supports. The operation was more streamlined this time, and Noel's assistants were trained to have a camera out of its box, assembled, and onto a tripod in 30 seconds.

CAPTAIN NOEL PREPARES TO FILM A RIVER CROSSING IN TIBET.

Noel filmed the rescue of the marooned porters by telephoto and spent nine and a half days on the North Col. From his "Eagle's Nest," he was able to film Mallory and Irvine at 26,000 feet from a distance of two miles. His summit-pyramid shots showed more detail of Everest's surface and its difficulties than ever before. As arranged with Mallory, he watched the summit for hours to see Mallory and Irvine on their last fateful climb, but there was no sign of them.

In this second film, *The Epic of Mount Everest,* Noel concentrated on portraying the character and power of the mountain and the insignificance of man. The reviewer from the *Bioscope* felt he succeeded, calling it "immeasurably fuller and finer in every respect" than his previous effort. "Thanks partly to the restrained, yet forcefully expressive subtitling, partly to the realistic illusion created by these wonderful pictures, one gains a very strong sense of the drama of the climb. With the baffled explorers one begins to fancy that this dreadful pile of rock, lowering demonically behind a veil of mist, is actually a living thing." Copies of both of Noel's films are now held by the National Film Archive in London.

felt unwell all day, and Irvine struggled with a headache, but managed to turn out to share some of the load-carrying with the struggling porters coming up. "They were almost too exhausted to walk without loads," he wrote that night. "At last we got them into camp and distributed the eight sleeping bags I was carrying and got a Primus going in one of their tents."

Mallory was in despair. Another day had passed with only a handful more loads making it to Camp III, and nothing done to improve the camp. He got up early again the next morning and descended once more to Camp II. There he met Norton and Somervell, who were surprised to see so many people in the camp. Mallory explained how, because of the men's suffering, he'd been obliged to initiate the load-dump at the head of the Trough. The news was received coolly. Geoffrey Bruce was later quite outspoken about the incident, calling it "a severe breakdown," and saying it "would undoubtedly have developed into a complete collapse of the porters had Norton not been present at the critical moment to keep them on their feet and restore their ebbing courage and spirits." The supply column was broken, something of which Noel, too, was critical. From then on, convoy parties started to choose their own sites for dumping, he said, so that the expedition's stores became scattered all along the line, and the whole transportation system crumpled.

The real trouble was that the master plan had made no allowance for bad weather, and the blizzards they were experiencing were some of the worst in 20 years. Whatever was thought of his decision, Mallory welcomed the arrival of

Mallory, in hat in the foreground, glanced at the camera during establishment of Camp II. Above rises Mount Kellas, at 23,331 feet, named for the physician who had died on the 1921 reconnaissance expedition.

Geoffrey Bruce, knowing he could pass the responsibility to him while he caught up on some sleep. Odell and Hazard, meanwhile, began prospecting a way up the col. Irvine, again fighting a headache, set about organizing Camp III and seeing to it that the porters got their primuses going and some hot food inside them. Somervell arrived with more porters.

"Perfectly bloody day—nothing else will describe it,"Irvine wrote on May 9th, and busied himself tinkering with the Roarer Cooker. Somervell and Odell decided the weather was too "filthy" to have another go at the Col; Hazard went down; Mallory, Noel, and Bruce came up. Mallory was surprised and pleased to be greeted in camp by "the cheery noise of the Roarer Cooker," which to his mind was one of the great inventions of the expedition. It was extravagent on fuel, a bit temperamental, and tended to frighten the cook, but it fed the troops. Everyone retreated to their tents. Two of the "Meades" had been pitched door to door so that Mallory, Somervell, Odell, and Irvine could share a "room," where they enjoyed a game of cards, read poetry, and waited for their wondrous cook, Kami, to produce the evening meal.

That night the wind gained even more force, and whatever precautions they took, fresh snow drifted into the tents, forming drifts inches thick in places. The scene in the morning was one of utter desolation, and

Experiencing "glacial lassitude" after the difficulties of setting up camps, expedition members rest among the ice pinnacles between Camps II and III (above). They straggled back to Base dejected (opposite) after being forced down by unexpectedly fierce storms and extreme cold.

Bruce was pressing for getting the porters down to base, while they still had their strength. Mallory though, still smarting from the suggestion that he capitulated too easily before, urged that they stay another day before making up their minds. He couldn't believe the weather would continue battering them with such force. It had to clear up soon, and they might get some work done in the afternoon. Nevertheless, they were burning too much fuel with so many Sahibs in camp and, as Irvine was still dogged by his headache and rheumatic pains, he and Mallory retreated to Camp II. "Found it difficult to keep up with George," Irvine wrote of the nightmare descent, "and the rough ice shook my head terribly." He had to rest every few minutes and any little undulation brought him to his knees. Mallory put it down to "glacier lassitude."

On the morning of the 11th, news was received at Camp II that, just above camp, a porter had fallen and broken his leg. Mallory, Irvine, Beetham, and Noel hurried out with a splint and makeshift stretcher to bring him down. Meanwhile, after another night of cold and gales at Camp III, Norton decided to order everyone off the mountain. Irvine, who was feeling better after a night at lower altitude, tramped uphill once more to fetch Somervell to minister to the injured man. Unfortunately,

this was not the only casualty. Another porter, Sanglu, one of Kellas's old hands, was suspected to have pneumonia, and the team's cobbler, Manbahadur, had been found in an apathetic condition lying out on the snow. He was carried down from Camp II, but it was clear he would lose both feet to frostbite.

Back at Base Camp, they found Hingston had returned, having left the general in better health. Bottles of champagne were opened to welcome him back, and Irvine looked around his companions. "A very dirty and bedraggled company," he concluded. "Hingston clean shaven and proper sitting opposite Shebbeare with a face like a villain and a balaclava inside out on the back of his head. Hazard in a flying helmet with a bristly chin sticking out further than ever. Beetham sat silent most of the time, round and black like a mixture of Judas Iscariot and an apple dumpling. George sitting on a very low chair could hardly be seen above the table except for a cloth hat pinned up on one side with a huge safety pin and covered with candle grease. Noel as usual leaning back with his chin down and cloth hat over his eyes, grinning to himself. Everyone very happy to be back in a Christian mess hut eating decent food."

Norton prepared his expedition dispatch. "The end of Round One finds us discomfited, but very far from defeated," he wrote, trying to put a brave face on what was little more than a rout. "A hitch, but by no means the crash we feared. We lose inevitably five or six days of the original programme....Give us but the weather encountered in 1922 and nothing will prevent the smooth continuance of the plan."

COL. E. F. NORTON, PHOTOGRAPHED IN 1924 BY HOWARD SOMERVELL AT 28,126 FEET. NO MOUNTAINEER WAS DOCUMENTED TO EXCEED HIS ELEVATION RECORD UNTIL 1952.

CHAPTER FIVE

...we expect no mercy from Everest.

GEORGE MALLORY, MAY 1924

THE LAMA'S BLESSING

Hingston had his work cut out for him. On May 12 he set off for Camp I to tend to casualties and was shocked at the "worn and weather-beaten crowd" he found there. "Completely done up...a sorry lot." The Nepalese cobbler with frostbite looked certain to lose both legs from the knees, and there were other cases of porters with frostbitten fingers or snow blindness. The man with the fractured leg was doing all right, but the sick Gurkha, Shamsher Pun, was unconscious with a suspected blood clot on the brain; he could not be moved and was left in the care of fellow NCOs. Hingston went up again to see him on the 13th, with Geoffrey Bruce. "A distressing day," his diary recalls, "We found him even worse than when we had left him. However we had to try and get him down." A stretcher was improvised from blankets and tent-poles, and six Tibetans were detailed to act as bearers for what proved a long and difficult carry. When they were within half a mile of base camp, Shamsher died without regaining consciousness. He was buried the next day across the river from base camp. "The death of this splendid young man in the prime of youth is much felt by the members of the expedition," Norton wrote in his dispatch that night, tendering his sympathies to the soldier's parents and regiment.

If anything was to be salvaged from this reversal, and spirit restored among the men, something had to be done. At no time had General Bruce been more sorely missed. The interpreter, Karma Paul, was sent down to the Rongbuk Monastery to ask if the porters could be blessed by the Head Lama there, a celebrated holy man said to be an incarnation of the God Chenrezi. This lama, Ngag-dwang-batem-hdsin-norbu, was a popular figure with all the early Everesters, greeting successive expeditions with the utmost courtesy from 1922 through the 1930s. He hit it off particularly well with General Bruce, who told him that his climbers were from a British mountain-worshipping sect on a pilgrimage to the highest mountain in the world. Bruce wanted to convey that their motives were entirely spiritual, and they were seeking no material gain by coming. After all, had not Chenrezi himself been to the holy snows on top of Chomolungma, according to legend, wafted there on a sunbeam? The Lama agreed to invite the whole expedition to the monastery on the 15th—climbers, Gurkhas, and porters. Accordingly, they all marched the four miles down into the valley at the appointed hour, to be shown first into an anteroom and offered Tibetan tea and bowls of spiced noodles. "Most of us loathed the stuff, but Noel had several helps," Hingston recorded. Irvine remarked on how well chewed the chopsticks were, and when they were finally ushered into the presence of the Head Lama, he noted that the great man was sitting "on a red throne on an iron bedstead just inside a kind of verandah." The Lama was said to have spent 12 years in a hermit's cell. He blessed every man by pressing a silver prayer wheel to his head. The deeply religious porters prostrated themselves in front of him before making their offerings of rupees and silk *khatas.* Norton presented their host with a silk embroidered picture of the Potala, the Dalai Lama's palace in Lhasa, and a watch. Prayers were said, and the Lama exhorted the porters to obey the sahibs and to do their best on the mountain. It was the demons who had forced them back, he said, and would try to do so again, but they must be strong. He would pray for them. The group trooped back to camp with renewed resolution.

When the expedition leaders met with the Head Lama of Rongbuk (right, center) they told him, "If we arrive at the summit we will get from the British government a recompense and high rank." The Lama considered the men heretics, but he showed them hospitality. Reported General Bruce, "We all parted on the most friendly terms."

Decades later, the Rongbuk Monastery would fall victim to the Cultural Revolution. When we arrived in Tibet with the first Mallory and Irvine Search Expedition in 1986, the once-imposing monastery was little more than a shell. A few nuns and a young lama had settled

among the ruins and were doing what they could to bring it back to life. One of our members, Tom Holzel, suggested that the monks may have kept some sort of monastery log or daybook, which, if it still existed, would perhaps mention the round-eyed foreigners who had come to climb the Goddess Mother in the 1920s. We took our interpreters to the monastery but found nothing. We did learn, however, that the Lama of Rongbuk had written his memoirs in which he recalled the British mountain climbers. The document survived the Cultural Revolution (presumably by being taken over the border to the sister monastery of Thyangboche in Nepal). A translation by Tibetan scholars was seen by Shebbeare soon after World War II, and he attached a copy of the relevant section to his Everest 1924 diary, which is lodged at the Alpine Club in London.

The white men, the old Lama had recorded, "pitched 7 tents in a row up the hill, and for about six weeks they tried to ascend the hill, taking iron pegs, chains and plates etc [axes, ropes, crampons] with them." It is not known when the Lama wrote this, but he appears to have fused events of 1924 and 1922 when he recalls "two big sahibs" being lost

(Mallory and Irvine, perhaps) at the same time as "seven or eight porters were killed." When asked to make funeral benedictions and blessings for the deceased persons, he had responded with "great keenness," he said, "also thinking that these souls suffered such great untold difficulties for the sake of nothing."

Upon return to camp, Norton and Bruce reworked their porter logistics, and Mallory, Odell, and Somervell tested their fitness by climbing outcrops of rock around camp. Irvine, as equipment officer, spent his days improvising and mending. His efforts during the expedition went beyond the call of duty. He repaired axes, stoves, torches, stools, tables, even Noel's camera motor. In camps across Tibet he had operated a mobile tinker's shop, and tapped and brazed into the night. His main concern was the oxygen outfit, which had been found (as he wrote to a friend) to be completely "boggled," when examined at Calcutta. No one at the manufacturers, Siebe Gorman, had taken notice of suggestions he'd sent to them in the months before their departure. What was sent was "hopeless, breaks if you touch it, leaks, is ridiculously clumsy and heavy." Out of 90 cylinders, he and Odell found that 15 were empty and 24 were leaking badly. "Ye Gods!" he wrote in exasperation. "I broke one yesterday taking it out of its packing

Like some fantastic stage set, the jagged ice pinnacles of the East Rongbuk Glacier's ice corridor frame the path to Everest. Here the corridor, created by glacial ice melting unevenly and sinking in the middle, seems headed for Mount Kellas. But the route eventually curves away toward Everest itself.

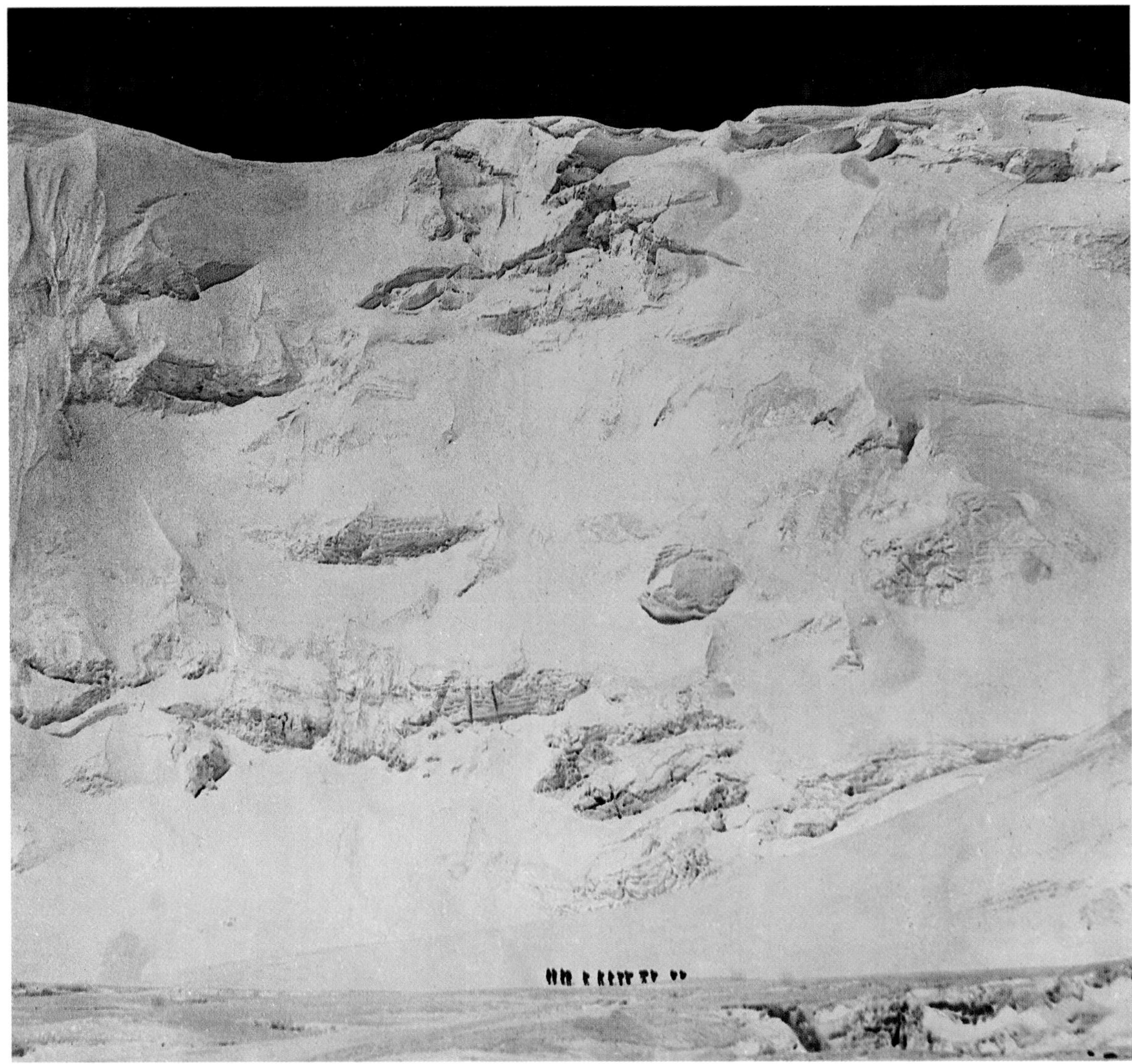

case." Though philosophically he would have preferred to climb without supplemental oxygen, Irvine set himself to repair the damage, at the same time reassembling some of the sets in a more practical manner. By the time he reached Shegar, he could display his Mark V prototype, which reversed the cylinders in their carrying frame and reduced the amount of pipework required to convey oxygen to the face mask. They tested it by climbing the rocks of the dzong. Once at base camp he struggled to get six of these newly designed sets and four of the original design ready for use. There are photographs of the camp with oxygen pack frames lying like carcasses in a charnel house.

Mallory itched from inactivity. "You'll be glad to hear," he wrote reassuringly to Ruth,

The North Col, a 1,000-foot wall of snow and ice dwarfs an expedition group headed for Camp IV, situated at the top of the wall, just behind its lip.

"that I came through the bad time unscathed—indeed excellently fit. I must tell *you* that with immense physical pride I look upon myself as the strongest of the lot, the most likely to get to the top with or without gas." Modesty demanded that he add, "I may be wrong," but he could not resist adding that he was pretty sure Norton felt the same. "He and I were agreeing yesterday that none of the new members, with the possible exception of Irvine, can touch the veterans and that the old gang are bearing everything on their shoulders." He was particularly disappointed that Odell and Hazard had failed to complete the reconnaissance of this year's route up the North Col and that Beetham had not regained his form. "It is an effort to pull oneself together and do what is required high up," he said, "but it is the power to keep the show going when you don't feel energetic that will enable us to win through if anything does. Irvine has much more of the winning spirit."

During this respite at base, Mallory was sharing a tent with Captain Noel who found him a restless companion. "He seemed ill at ease, always scheming and planning," Noel remembered. "It was obvious to me he felt this setback more acutely than any of us." At length it was decided to stick to their earlier program from the North Col upward, just postponing it by 12 days so that "Ascension Day," as Mallory liked to call it, would coincide with the Ascension Day of the Christian calendar, May 29 that year. They now knew which of their porters were likely to perform best, and there was as yet no reason to suspect their chances of success were significantly diminished. "I feel strong for the battle but I know every ounce of strength will be wanted," Mallory told Ruth. And to his sister Mary, who was diligently sending details of the weather in Ceylon, he apologized that the chances of having time to see her after the expedition were "disappearing down the Tibetan wind."

On May 17 the struggle was resumed—the day on which they had originally planned to stand on the summit. "Not a cloud on the mountain till 11 a.m.," Irvine observed wryly as he went about all the odd jobs required in getting the first five men back up the glacier. "Perfect climbing day, no wind early. What a pity!"

He followed in their footsteps the next day, though feeling "rather rotten" from a dose of diarrhea. The weather had closed in again; in fact in the afternoon it looked to Irvine "a very dirty day on the mountain." He only made it as far as Camp I, where he took some lead and opium in the hope of improvement and settled down for a long night in a comfortably large sleeping bag, and felt a lot better for it.

By the 21st, Somervell, Hazard, and Irvine finally established Camp IV on the North Col, in the same position as in 1922. Not a trace of the old camp remained. Hazard was detailed to remain up there in charge of 12 porters, while the others turned back down through thickening snowfall. A blizzard raged all that night, and it was still snowing and windy the next day. It was impossible for Odell to bring up the next party of bearers and to relieve Hazard, as planned. The night of May 22-23 produced the lowest temperature recorded during the whole expedition, minus 24°F—worse than on their previous high trip. The cold firmed up the new snow, and the following morning, under pressure to keep the "show" going and not let any more precious days slip by, Bruce and Odell set off up the slopes with a party of 16 loaded porters.

Meanwhile, on the Col, Hazard and his men were having a bleak time, so it was with relief that he observed, "sometime in the late forenoon" of the 23rd, a large party of 18 to 20 members moving between Camp III and the base of the North Col. At last, Hazard thought, at last! A day late, but here is the party that will take over from me at Camp IV and go on to establish Camp V, for that had been the arrangement. Concluding that there would be scant room on the Col for both groups to occupy the same camp that night without great discomfort and depletion of stores, Hazard decided to evacuate his men before the relief party reached him. He detailed two porters to remain behind and prepare a meal for the arriving party in accordance with Norton's

Norton and Somervell get to sit, but the porters behind them are the ones who accomplished a phenomenal physical feat: They carried a full load of equipment to establish Camp VI at the 26,800-foot level. Norbu Yishay, Lhakpa Chedi, and Semchumbi assisted Norton and Somervell in their failed attempt to reach Everest's summit.

THE SHERPAS

The person credited with first employing Sherpas for high mountain work was Dr. Alexander Kellas. In the years preceding the early Everest expeditions, he explored widely in Sikkim and other parts of the Himalaya, climbing, indeed often traversing, virgin snow peaks of over 20,000 feet with his band of trained Sherpas. Fit, hard, loyal, and almost impervious to cold, these men carried enormous loads and, for the most part, remained infectiously cheerful. It made them a natural choice for the higher altitudes of Everest, although precisely how much higher they would be able to go was unknown. On the reconnaissance of 1921, they were not asked to go much above 20,000 feet; that year the high point was the North Col at 21,000 feet, which three porters and their sahibs reached. Howard-Bury reported afterward that "the Sherpa Bhotia proved a very useful and capable type of man, who could be rapidly trained in snow and ice craft, and who was not afraid of the snow or cold."

PORTERS RECEIVING THEIR "KIT" AT SHEGAR DZONG

In 1922, Bruce's Darjeeling agent, M. Wetherall, had gathered 150 likely applicants, from which a preselection of 75 of the best was made. This group was hospitalized for three days, examined, and treated for worms. Then the pick of them were chosen for the trip.

The problem facing General Bruce was to bring his elite porters, destined to go to high altitude, to Advance Base without deterioration. In this he succeeded, at the same time appealing to their spirit and instilling in them a sense of the honor they would share in if the venture were successful. Supplying them with good food, good pay, and reasonable kit helped in wedding them to the expedition's purpose. The bond proved so successful that, ever after, few expeditions to the high peaks of Tibet and Nepal were undertaken without Sherpa assistance. Even after the avalanche disaster of 1922, in which at least two of the Sherpa porters lost brothers and others their special friends, Bruce said that not one of the men showed any desire not to return; in fact, every single one of them signed up for the next expedition.

After the 1922 trip, Mallory reported that the greatest lesson learned was that the Sherpas' power far exceeded anyone's expectations. They carried loads to 25,500 feet, and some of them even could repeat this amazing accomplishment on three successive days, showing remarkably little fatigue. There was no reason to suppose that they could not carry even higher, maybe to 27,000 feet. As yet, he stressed, this power was not allied to skill or experience, but such reservations changed over the years, as Sherpa porters became familiar with their territory and the needs of a climbing expedition. Many expeditions now employ Sherpas in much the manner of Alpine guides, to show the way forward.

The Sherpa homeland is the Solu Khumbu region of Nepal, an area of high valleys to the south and west of Mount Everest, close to the border with Tibet. But Sherpas are of Tibetan origin, having crossed into Nepal some four centuries ago. Their name comes from Shar-pa, meaning "people from the east." Many of the Sherpas employed by the early Everest expeditions lived in Darjeeling (India), because work was more plentiful there. They were known as Bhotias, but their family ties with Nepal remained strong. General Bruce said at Base Camp in 1922, Sherpa porters were visited by relations from across the border. They came up from the Solu Khumbu, across the Nangpa La (or Khumbu La) at 19,000 feet, and then up to base camp. Some of the wives carried babies as young as six months old over the pass, sleeping under rocks for shelter.

In 1924, after bad weather and a series of setbacks, several porters were out with frostbite, exhaustion, or simple discouragement. But the fittest among them were rallied to go high again. These were the "tigers" of whom great things were expected. Though there was little enthusiasm among the tigers, several began ascending. Norton used his persuasive powers to keep them going, pointing out that honor and glory would be theirs if they carried loads higher than any Sherpa had done before. Whether they believed him or not, three of the tigers—Norbu Yishay, Lhakpa Chedi and Semchumbi—showed their mettle and went on to install the high camp.

It was not until after the British Everest Expedition of 1938 that a superior grade for Sherpa and Bhotia porters—those who had distinguished themselves by going to the highest levels—was officially recognized. Awarded a bronze Tiger Medal, they qualified for higher rates of pay above the snow line. Becoming a tiger was what young Sherpas aspired to for many years, particularly after the successful ascent of Everest in 1953 by Edmund Hillary and Sherpa Tenzing Norgay. At that time, the word "Sherpa" entered Western consciousness and folklore as signifying fortitude and reliability.

The Sherpas have paid heavily for their involvement with the world's highest mountains. From the first climbing expedition, which robbed seven of their lives, Sherpa fatalities have been disproportionately higher than those of their employers. Of the first hundred people who died on Everest, 41 were Sherpas.

PORTERS LEAVING ADVANCE BASE CAMP ON THEIR WAY TO THE NORTH COL

strict ideas about supporting climbers after arduous activity. As the only sahib in his party, Hazard went ahead to fix a rope handrail to safeguard his charges down the perilously slumped slopes of the col.

Sometime at the beginning of the second stage of "this centipede progression," two more men decided to return to the relative comfort and safety of Camp IV. Hazard only learned this when the rest of the team assembled at the start of the third traverse. By then, he could see the two had regained camp without mishap, and had no particular concern on their behalf. He continued down with the rest of his men.

By the time they collected at the base of the ice chimney, the major barrier of the route, mist had enveloped them and the light was bad. Worse still, they were dismayed, in a brief clearing of the mist, to see the relieving party had turned back. No amount of shouting could catch their attention. When Hazard reached Camp III at 5:00 that evening, it was snowing once more.

Norton's relief at seeing the column come safely down through worsening weather was rudely shattered on learning that four men were "marooned" at Camp IV, with precious little food apart from a sack of barley meal. The snow, falling wet and heavy, convinced Norton that the monsoon was already upon them. Every effort had to be made to rescue the stranded men the next morning, especially as one of them was already displaying signs of frostbite. Despite Norton's earnest intention that there should be no casualties this year, he could see another catastrophe looming—and this at a time when, back at base, Manbahadur, the man frostbitten earlier in the month, was losing his long battle for his life.

Once more Norton ordered his troops off the mountain. He, Mallory, and Somervell would risk the avalanche slopes the next morning in a bid to reach the stranded men. Irvine would not be fit enough to join them, and they would miss his brute strength. In truth, none of them was up to par. Mallory had a racking cough, and Somervell was plagued with a feverish "high altitude throat." "Were men ever faced with such a task?" Geoffrey Bruce has written. What if they failed to bring off a rescue; what if they found some of the marooned men frostbitten and unable to move? He worried that the superstitious porters might be frightened to the point of hurling themselves down the ice slopes. Indeed, after the rescue, these porters told him that during their night alone on the North Col they had distinctly heard the fierce barking of the watchdogs guarding the Goddess' abode.

Mallory, in his writings, makes no mention of barking dogs, but he could barely sleep for coughing. He and Norton were encouraged in the early part of the night, however, to see the moon come out. And the snow had stopped. It was not the monsoon then, not this time, but the col's slopes were dangerously heavy with moist, sticky snow. "Never, I confess," Mallory afterward wrote, "has a task appeared to my mind so utterly far away and unlikely to be accomplished." Next morning, as they straggled across the knee-deep snow of the basin toward the col, sick and cold, it seemed to him that they were "like a party of thrashed curs." Irvine crossed his fingers for them, took a large dose of castor oil, and headed off down the glacier with Geoffrey Bruce.

The rescue team made its way apprehensively upward, Norton and Somervell taking turns to break trail while the other two belayed. Approaching the final slopes, they were able to shout to the marooned men. "Are you ready to move?" The poor men had no idea if their masters desired them to move up or to move down, and were delighted to learn they could descend. It was already 4:30 in the afternoon before Somervell reached them—or rather, he almost reached them, for the rope was just too short to allow him to step up to their ledge. He did not want to remove the rope, as it would serve as a handrail for the descending men; they would need to slide down the few feet to reach him. In their haste, two of the porters slipped and began sliding down the slope, toward the ice cliffs. Only the buildup of plowed snow ahead of them halted their progress. But they were too terrified to move. Mallory and Norton watched with mounting horror, but Somervell stayed calm. They should stay where they were, not to stir an inch, while he passed the others who had made it to him safely along the line. Then he took off the rope, belayed it to his ax, and in a few moments gathered the errant porters "to his bosom in a paternal manner worthy of Abraham"—so it struck Mallory. These two were then passed down the rope in turn. Namgya, the man with the frostbitten hands, was able to walk under his own steam, but had a hard time coming down the fixed rope in the ice chimney.

At last all were safely at the foot of the cliff, to be met by Noel, Odell, and three porters with thermos flasks of hot soup. "They will deserve their thrones in heaven," remarked Mallory. So, too, did the three of them for their gallantry that day. Longstaff, writing up the incident for an Indian newspaper, made sure his readers knew what was entailed: "Talk about pulling the whiskers of Death—these folk crawled in through the chinks between his closed teeth! None of the three expected to come out of it alive."

But where did the rescue leave their plans for the mountain? The monsoon could be little more than a week away now. A month had passed since their arrival in Base Camp and twice they had been rebuffed. Not a step had been taken above the North Col; three of the strongest climbers had been seriously weakened in the rescue effort, and the only "plumb fit" man, as Mallory now told Ruth, was Geoffrey Bruce. The team gathered in Camp I on May 27 for a council of war.

Norton proposed abandoning the oxygen attempt all together and concentrating porter power in getting two higher camps installed and all camps properly supplied. He reckoned they could count on only 15 of their porters to keep going now—the corps of "Tigers," as they would henceforth be known. Shebbeare suggested that since some of the nonclimbers were now the fittest of the bunch, as a last resource they could be drafted into the climbing team. Norton squashed the proposal firmly; he had

Irvine built a rope ladder to aid porters in carrying loads to the North Col, at 23,000 feet. The team had previously hauled loads hand-over-hand.

no wish to rescue any more men from the snow and ice of the North Col.

Norton's modified plan found favor with everyone except Mallory, who saw the opportunity of anyone gaining the summit slipping away. "All sound plans are now abandoned for two consecutive dashes without gas," he vented his frustration to David Pye, telling him that the "old gangers"—Norton, Somervell, and himself—were to go first. Although he had always wanted to climb without oxygen, now with time at a premium, he resented the extra day a gasless attempt would need. "If the monsoon lets us start from Camp IV, it will almost certainly catch us on one of the *three* days from there. Bright prospects!" And to Ruth he wrote, "Dear girl, this has been a bad time altogether... I look back on tremendous efforts and exhaustion and dismal looking out of a tent door onto a world of snow and vanishing hopes. And yet, and yet, and yet there have been a good many things to set on the other side. The party has played up wonderfully."

It fell to Mallory to choose the teams for the assaults. Norton had told him to include himself in the first party if he wanted, though Mallory professed now to Ruth that he felt unsure he'd be fit enough, or if the monsoon would give them a chance. We can see he was breaking the news gently to her, as he always did, for the letter soon reveals that he sees there is a chance and wants to seize it. "Six days to the top from this camp!" With this realization, he immediately begins working out the likeliest pairings to bring them success. That night, by the time his candle burned low and he wound up his letter, there was no doubt in his mind. "Darling, I wish you the best I can that your anxiety will be at an end before you get this, with the best news, which will always be the quickest," he wrote. "It is fifty to one against us but we'll have a whack yet and do ourselves proud. Great love to you, ever your loving George."

"Another precious day of fine weather was sacrificed on the 28th to the recuperation of the climbers," wrote Norton in his dispatches. Even so the climbers began dribbling back up the line. Irvine went to Camp II, where he used the time to construct a rope ladder to assist loaded porters in negotiating the difficult ice chimney section on the cliff of the North Col. Every third rung was made of wood—a picket, a tent peg, anything that could be mustered—to give some rigidity to the structure. It took a lot of splicing, which was excruciatingly hard on the fingers, but Odell and Shebbeare lent a hand. The ladder's construction took all afternoon and most of the next day, but, "Like all the work of the well-known firm of 'Odell and Irvine,' this proved a most complete success," Norton reported.

It now seemed that the longed-for good weather was at last there. Day after day, the mountain stood "clear-cut in azure," Norton wrote, with even its characteristic streamer-cloud absent. All indications that the monsoon was about to break had vanished. Most of the party was back at Camp III by the last day of the month, including Captain Noel and his "kinema outfit." Even Beetham had hobbled up against doctor's orders, but he had such an acute case of sciatica that Norton straightaway ordered him back, telling him to send up the doctor instead. He would be more useful.

Accompanied by 9 of their 15 "Tigers," Mallory and Geoffrey Bruce camped on the North Col ready to move higher the next morning, June 1. Odell and Irvine went with them in support. It still appeared fine when the two climbers and eight of their porters set off next day to climb the North Ridge and establish Camp V. However, Camp IV was situated among the jumble of crevasses and seracs up against Changtse, at the opposite end to the ridge, and no sooner had they stepped out on the col than a bitter and penetrating northwest wind struck them from the side and stayed with them all day. Before reaching the site for Camp V (200 feet above Mallory's 1922 Camp V, on the east side of the ridge), half of the porters had dumped their loads, unable to go further. While Mallory leveled out tent platforms, Bruce and the strongest remaining Sherpa, Lobsang Bhote, made two trips down and up 300 feet to retrieve the dumped packs.

"Two fragile little tentlets perched on an almost precipitous slope"—was how Norton afterward described this new camp; not a secure, welcoming spot by any means, but at least it offered shelter from the killing wind. Morale remained low, however, and next morning, despite Bruce's earnest cajoling,

A raging wind from the west slams into the 1,000-foot wall below Camp IV—and is deflected skyward, obscuring a view of Mount Changtse. Despite the howling wind beyond, the tents of Camp IV barely ripple. Such protective barriers don't exist farther up the mountain, where climbers face nature's fiercest elements head-on.

three more of the porters could not be persuaded to continue. Instead of this being their summit day, Mallory had to send a note down to Norton: "Show's crashed—wind took the heart of our porters yesterday and none will face going higher today....We are staying for the present to improve the camp, make the 3rd emplacement and perhaps, if you have better luck than us, you will be able to establish VI tomorrow." Before long, Mallory and Bruce followed their Sherpas back to the Col. Halfway down, they met the second assault team, Norton and Somervell, coming up with their six porters.

Once again reality had fallen short of Mallory's imagining. If the second team succeeded in putting in Camp VI, he was sure that was all they could do. He still believed the consecutive "dashes" without gas were unlikely to yield them the summit. It came back to the old question of oxygen: He was convinced now that the "English Air" offered them their only hope. Tired as he was, already a new plan was formulating in his mind.

Norton and Somervell left the North Col at 6:00 that morning, June 2nd, after a good night's sleep—"Beds of snow are much more comfortable than those of the stones at the

camp below," Somervell remarked—and were sent on their way by a breakfast cooked by Irvine. They, too, caught the full blast of the wind crossing the snowy shoulder of the Col, but pulled their fur caps down over their ears, tightened their belts, and stomped as fast as the altitude would allow, so as not to get chilled. It was a disappointment to see Mallory and Bruce returning so soon, and they became anxious over their own porters. Would they too be unable or unwilling to go above Camp V? But no, sending two back after delivering their loads to Camp V, the other four camped in one of the tiny tents, with the two climbers in the other. A good meal of pemmican and bully beef, followed by coffee and biscuits, helped restore them and, according to Somervell, they passed "a very fair night, during at least half of which we slept, finding no discomfort from the altitude or difficulty in breathing."

The fine weather held, and three of the porters were willing next morning to carry loads onward. It was a weary plod on loose scree, which at 26,700 feet gave way to the infamous sloping slabs of the North Face, with their coating of little pebbles. They found a rocky little basin and settled on that for a campsite. "Far from ideal," Somervell wrote, "but...on Everest you have got to take what you can get and be thankful." The porters were sent back with a note giving instructions that they were to be well fed that night for their sterling service. But the sahibs themselves had no appetite; coffee and soup were all they could eat. They filled the thermos for breakfast to save time in the morning, but it leaked in the night, and they had to brew the coffee anyway and did not get away until about 6:45 a.m. Norton and Somervell struck out diagonally to the right, lured by the first patch of sunlight. There were snowy patches that Norton chipped his way across, and at last they reached the distinctive band of yellow limestone that encircles the mountain. The rock was weathered into comfortably wide horizontal ledges, offering easy enough going, though it was breathtaking work.

The world is at the frozen feet of Colonel Norton, who sits trying to catch his breath at the 27,800-foot level in a little-known photograph by Somervell. His view from this point was very similar to the the view also photographed by Somervell (following pages), at nearly the same elevation. Climbing without oxygen, Norton also went without goggles, mistakenly assuming that he would not suffer snow blindness in the absence of snow. The blazing high-altitude sun, however, left him seeing double and then he went snowblind.

The effects of altitude were beginning to tell. From about 27,500 ft some eight or ten respirations were required for every step made, and even then the two men were bent over their axes, gasping, after every few yards. Another 500 feet of height was gained before Somervell felt too weak to continue. His sore throat was agony; it had been getting worse for days, ever since the porter rescue, and nothing heals at altitude. He urged Norton to push on without him, and settled on a rock to watch his progress.

It was at this moment that Somervell took one of the most poignant photographs of Everest history (page 144)—the tiny, lone figure of Norton, at 28,128 feet, cautiously picking

his way over steep and virgin snow-coated slabs, with the white summit pyramid luring him on.

"But Norton himself was not far from the end of his tether," Somervell observed. "I watched him rise, but how slowly, and after an hour I doubt whether he had risen 80 ft above my level."

It was a fine, bright day, though bitterly cold. Norton wasn't moving fast enough to keep warm and, frightened of making any false moves, he had taken off his goggles to see his footing more clearly. It was a serious mistake. By afternoon he was experiencing double vision; on the next day he would be completely snowblind. He kept to the top edge of the Yellow Band, making for the Great Couloir, which slashes the North Face (and is now as commonly known as Norton's Couloir). Two buttresses of rock had to be circumvented before the Couloir itself could be entered. Here the going became infinitely more difficult, often appearing to offer nothing firm at all beneath the feet. Yet, strangely, this is just the sort of terrain with which Norton was most familiar. His grandfather had a chalet in the Swiss Alps, the Eagle's Nest, on very similar loose ground to this; and many were the boyhood holidays Norton spent scrambling around there with his family. But today the strain was telling and the slabs were pitched steeply, like tiles on a roof. Crossing the Couloir was no easy matter as it was choked with deep, powdery snow. Beyond, "the going got steadily worse; I found myself stepping from tile to tile, as it were, each tile sloping more steeply downwards." It was, he decided, too dangerous a place for a single, unroped climber. One slip could pitch him into an uncontrollable tumbling fall.

Looking down on Everest's west ridge, Somervell photographed a vista that included Pumori (23,507 feet, at center), Cho Oyu (26,906 feet, at upper right), and the West Rongbuk Glacier (far right).

Time, moreover, was running out. Though the summit pyramid looked tantalizingly close, only another 200 feet of climbing above him, he could see it wouldn't be possible to get there and back in daylight. Displaying admirable good sense and restraint, he turned and retraced his steps to rejoin Somervell. His high point was later calculated to be 28,126 feet.

"So with heavy hearts, beating over 180 to the minute, we returned," wrote Somervell, though even climbing downhill was hard work. The views were magnificent, "a vast array of peak upon peak," but they were not at their most appreciative. In his tiredness Somervell lost grip of his ice ax, which clanged and cartwheeled down the slabs. At Camp VI they stopped only long enough to pack rucksacks; at Camp V, where the going became safer, the pair unroped and, as they found their own pace, inevitably separated. Norton was soon glissading to get down more quickly. When his partner failed to keep up, he thought that he had "stopped to sketch or photograph the effect of the sunset glow." In fact, Somervell was fighting for his life.

A paroxysm of coughing had dislodged something in his throat, so that he could neither breathe in nor out. Nor could he shout to

attract Norton's attention. "This is the end," he thought, sinking into the snow. With one last effort, he clasped both hands to his chest and pressed hard. Somervell, a man of great strength, gave "one last almighty push" and hawked out the obstruction. He supposed it to have been the entire mucous lining of his larynx, damaged by frostbite. Though still coughing up blood, he was relieved to find he could breathe more freely than he had for days.

By the time he caught up with Norton it was almost dark, and they picked their way to the North Col by the light of their torches. Mallory and Odell were there with lanterns to meet them and guide them through the crevasses into camp; Irvine brewed tea and soup. What a contrast to their "homecoming" in 1922 when they were greeted by an empty, foodless camp. Within an hour, they were fed, warmed, and asleep. "Norton is still recovering from severe snow-blindness," Somervell recalled a few days later, "...I can almost speak aloud again. We are both rather done in....There is nothing to complain of...we had a gorgeous day for the climb, almost windless and brilliantly fine, yet were unable to get to the summit. So we have no excuse—we have been beaten in fair fight; beaten by the height of the mountain, and by our own shortness of breath. But the fight was worth it, worth it every time, and we shall cherish the privilege of defeat by the world's greatest mountain."

THE NORTHEAST RIDGE OF EVEREST

CHAPTER SIX

The issue will shortly be decided. The third time we walk up East Rongbuk Glacier will be the last, for better or worse. We have counted our wounded and know, roughly, how much to strike off the strength of our little army as we plan the next act of battle.

GEORGE MALLORY, MAY 1924

INTO THE MISTS

The supreme effort of hauling loads during the installation of Camp V had distended Geoffrey Bruce's heart by two-and-a-half ribs, incapacitating him for high work. But Mallory came down from that first assault inwardly raging at their failure to get higher. Again, it seemed to him too early to turn back, too easy. Without waiting to see how Norton and Somervell fared, he immediately set to planning a third assault. This time he would climb with young Irvine, as he had always intended, and with oxygen, to take advantage of whatever mercurial wings that bag of tricks offered.

Irvine was bitterly disappointed at being left out of the summit dashes. "Feel very fit tonight," he wrote in his diary on May 30, "I wish I was in the first party instead of a bloody reserve." On the North Col three days later he was surprised to see Mallory and Bruce making their way back so soon. He hastily lit a couple of primuses, grabbed a rope and went to meet them on the col. George, he saw, was looking very tired.

Nevertheless, the pair lost no time in discussing Mallory's idea for an oxygen attempt and agreed to go down to Camp III that very afternoon to make the necessary preparations. The weather was still fine, and it looked as if Norton's belief that there were always ten days of clear weather before the monsoon was being confirmed. Though rested, Irvine was becoming badly burned from the high-altitude sun, reflected off the snows of the Col. "Face badly caught by the sun and wind," his diary records that day, "and my lips are cracked to bits, which makes eating very unpleasant." It was even worse that night, "Everything on earth seemed to rub against my face, and each time it was touched bits of burnt and dry skin came off, which made me nearly scream with pain." The prospect of climbing with a rubber face mask could not have been one he cared to think about, but Irvine made no complaint.

The hardest part was not knowing the outcome of the second assault. Odell was expected to come down to Camp III if Norton and Somervell returned on the 3rd, but he made no appearance. As Mallory and Irvine were assembling what they would need the next morning, word came that Camp VI was established, and that the climbers had overnighted there. Great excitement swept through the team. Noel set up his camera with the long telephoto lens, and everyone else remained glued to field glasses, hoping for a glimpse of the climbing pair. But there was no sign all day. "After an early tiffin," Irvine wrote, "George and I put the worst aspect on things, and we decided to go up to the North Col and be ready to fetch sick men down, or make an oxygen attempt ourselves a day later."

At Base Camp, Irvine works on the oxygen tanks. As he unpacked the tanks, shipped from England, he was aghast at what he found. "Out of 90 cylinders," he wrote a friend, "15 were empty and 24 leaked badly by the time they got to Calcutta. Ye Gods! I broke one today taking it out of its packing case."

Going up, they breathed supplemental oxygen part of the way, which, even at the low flow rate of 1.5 liters a minute, delivered them to Camp IV surprisingly fresh, and in a record time of two-and-a-half hours. Still nothing had been seen of the climbers higher on the mountain, though Mallory thought he could make out downward tracks some 700 feet below the summit. "I hope they've got to the top," Irvine wrote, "but by God, I'd like to have a whack at it myself."

At 8 p.m., Norton and Somervell were at last spotted coming down and were escorted back into camp, both very exhausted. That was it; the summit remained untrodden, and the third assault would leave the following morning.

Meanwhile, there was an air of foreboding down at Camp III, where nothing had been heard of Norton and Somervell since Camp VI was established. People were beginning to fear the worst. But then, on the evening of June 5, Somervell trudged into camp, disheveled and voiceless. Norton, he reported, was completely snowblind and had had to be left in Camp IV. As medical officer, Hingston resolved to go up the Col first thing in the morning to see what he could do to help; he had only just been freed of his base-camp duties and had moved up the line to be ready in the event of frostbites

among descending climbers. His was a humanitarian mission, and at the same time it was his personal introduction to Alpine mountaineering. Having never expected to get so high, the ascent struck him as "very wonderful," especially "the beautiful tints of green and blue shining out from the depths of ice."

When he reached the camp with its walls of ice, he found a dazzle of strong white glare and no place for a snowblind man. The others had covered Norton's tent with sleeping bags to keep it dark inside, but the leader was fretting to get down. He feared his presence at Camp IV could only be an "embarrassment" to Odell and Hazard, whose role now was to support Mallory and Irvine. "Hingston, being unable to perform the miracle of restoring my sight for the moment," Norton wrote later, "performed, with the help of Hazard and the two porters, another miracle....They shepherded me down some 1500 ft of sheer ice and snow, placing my every footstep, leading me by the hand, and supporting me with ropes, fixed and unfixed, with complete security. Hazard turned back after roping me from the top of the chimney to the bottom, and Hingston saw me the rest of the way into III."

Mallory's was not so much a bull-dog tenacity, or sheer hard determination to conquer, Younghusband later wrote, as "the imagination of the artist who cannot leave his work until it is completely, neatly and perfectly finished." To get him away from Everest before Everest itself had hurled him back, he said, "you would have had to pull him by the very roots of his being."

Norton professed himself "delighted" at the prospect of a third assault. Personally, he would have preferred Mallory make the attempt with Odell, who was vastly more experienced than young Irvine, but he could see why George and Sandy should want to be in this together. Irvine's familiarity with the oxygen apparatus was only part of it. The two had been linked as a probable ascent pair from the beginning, and Mallory had worked hard throughout the expedition at creating a keen esprit between them. Norton knew better than to challenge a decision already made, and besides, as he said, "Mallory was leader of the climbing party and organizing his own show, while I was a blind crock." He wished them well, but he suspected Mallory was aware he was leading a forlorn hope.

On the morning of Friday, June 6, Odell got up early to cook breakfast. A "choice fry of sardines," biscuits, and hot chocolate were served at the door of Mallory and Irvine's tent by Odell and Hazard. "They seemed pleased enough," Odell noted, regretting only that "they hardly did justice to the repast." Mallory was clearly impatient to be off, but it did not strike Odell that Irvine was any less determined to go "all out" for what they all recognized as the "culminating challenge." Odell's main reservation about the pair was that they were taking oxygen, of which he had never been a fan. He had failed to gain any advantage from it himself, and even blamed it for aggravating the sore throats from which Mallory and Irvine both suffered.

At 8:40 a.m., Odell pulled out his camera and immortalized the moment of departure,

Stranded on the North Col and rescued by Mallory, Norton, and Somervell, this porter, Namgya, was treated for frostbite and suffered no permanent damage. Namgya's badly swollen fingers actually signify a mild case of frostbite.

not knowing that it would be the last photograph ever taken of the pair: Mallory, facing the camera, is fiddling with his oxygen apparatus, as Irvine stands waiting, hands stuffed in pockets. Both have on their windproof jackets, breeches, and cashmere puttees. Mallory wore his air-force helmet with the flaps turned up, goggles, woolly scarf, and mitts; and Irvine, his brimmed hat. The climber's personal loads, each weighing about 28 or 29 pounds, consisted of their oxygen apparatus (as modified by Irvine), each with two cylinders, a few spare clothes, and provisions. Irvine had constructed a lightweight day bag from one of the cannibalized oxygen carriers, that he'd lent to Bruce during the first attempt, but it is not clear from Odell's snapshot whether he had it with him on the last climb. Eight Sherpas set out with them, carrying sleeping bags for all the men, fuel, and supplies. The porters would climb without the benefit of the "English Air."

With a brief farewell to still sightless Norton, who could only press their hands and wish them Godspeed, they were off. The day was fine, and the party reached Camp V in good time, where four porters were sent back to the col. They returned with a note from Mallory, which read "There is no wind here and things look hopeful."

The remaining porters returned from Camp VI the following afternoon, carrying two messages—pages torn from Mallory's notebook.

One was for Odell, and was delivered to him at Camp V, where he'd climbed with porter Nema to provide support to Mallory and Irvine. "We're awfully sorry to have left things in such a mess—our Unna cooker rolled down the slope at the last moment," the note said. "Be sure of getting back to IV tomorrow in time to evacuate before dark as I hope to. In the tent I must have left a compass—for the Lord's sake rescue it; we are without. To here on 90 atmospheres for the two days—so we'll probably go on two cylinders—but it's a bloody load for climbing. Perfect weather for the job."

As Nema was showing symptoms of mountain sickness, Odell scribbled his own note to Hazard and sent Nema back with the other porters, observing that the porter underwent a miraculous recovery as soon as he knew he would be heading down.

Mallory's second note was for Captain Noel, who was spending the day on the North Col, before going down to man the camera at his "Eagle's Nest" viewpoint, from where he had a good line of sight with the summit. Noel and Mallory had previously spoken of the most likely place the climbers might be spotted by the filmmaker on their epic attempt. "We'll probably start early tomorrow (8th) in order to have clear weather," Mallory had written. "It won't be too early to start looking out for us either crossing the rockband under the pyramid or going up skyline at 8 p.m." (He meant to write 8 a.m., of course.) Noel spoke with Lakpa, who had brought the message down, and was told that the Sahibs were well and the weather fine. It was Noel's conviction that Mallory intended to move the Camp VI tent that day, from 26,800 feet to 27,000 feet, and understood from Lakpa that this removal had been successfully achieved. None of the other accounts mention such a removal, nor is it generally accepted historically although, curiously, Odell, when he later arrived at Camp VI, did place the tent at 27,000 feet in his reports, remarking that the little mountain tent was "perched on a ledge, backed by steep rocks, by no means conspicuous or easy to find."

Meanwhile, Odell was enjoying his time at Camp V. "Wonderful time alone," his diary records, "and most gorgeous cloud effects on all mountains and far north into Thibet. Very calm." He had climbed to the camp in three-and-a-half hours without oxygen and felt

absolutely fine. Odell had undergone a miraculous transformation over the past week. From being a slow acclimatizer, he was now supremely fit and showing remarkable altitude adaptation. That evening, he sat at his tent door, entranced as the setting sun bathed a "savagely wild jumble of peaks" in "pinks and yellows of most exquisite tints," as his geographer's curiosity sought to identify and name as many of the peaks as possible. He did not mind being on his own, and in fact welcomed the opportunity to make a wide-ranging geological survey of the North Face on his way up to Camp VI the next day. He felt optimistic about Mallory's and Irvine's chances.

Odell was up at dawn, anxious to begin his survey. The business of getting ready, however, was laborious. Odell had no means of warming food or producing water as the high altitude cooker had been lost from this camp. There was no other stove in camp. As Odell later said of the loss, it "meant cold supper and breakfast for me!" He dined off tinned tomatoes and macaroni and "Force," a dry porridge meant to be mixed with water, which he in fact mixed with a little jam. The meager breakfast provided him with precious little liquid. We now know

This 1922 panoramic shot of Advance Base Camp shows the North Col sweeping like a white hammock between Changtse and Mount Everest. The summit of Everest is visible as a pyramid behind the closer Northeast Shoulder. Two years after this picture was taken the 1924 expedition's final attempt to conquer Everest would be launched from this same location.

that at least eight pints a day should be consumed at high altitude to prevent the effects of dehydration. Odell faced a remarkably heavy day with nothing at all to drink.

Unfortunately, the morning did not prove as fair as last evening's cloud display had led Odell to hope. By the time he left his tent at 8 o'clock, rolling banks of mist were sweeping across the face of the mountain from the west bringing with them flurries of sleet or light snow. But the wind had no bite, and from a certain luminosity in the sky, he felt sure that conditions higher up were probably comparatively clear. He had no qualms about Mallory or Irvine; they should be making good progress and might even be cutting steps up the final pyramid. He left the ridge and wandered on to the face. At about 26,000 feet he climbed a little crag, which he said afterward could easily have been bypassed. It rose about a hundred feet, and as he reached the top, the mists above him drifted apart to reveal the upper slopes of the mountain.

Odell's diary records merely that at 12:50 p.m. he "saw M & I on ridge, nearing base of final pyramide," but he expands upon the circumstances of his momentous sighting in his Mount Everest Dispatch, published in *The Times* on July 5, 1924: "At 12:50, just after I had emerged in a state of jubilation at finding the first definite fossils on Everest, there was a sudden clearing of the atmosphere, and the entire summit ridge and final peak of Everest were unveiled. My eyes became fixed on one tiny black spot silhouetted on a small snowcrest beneath a rock-step in the ridge, and the black spot moved. Another black spot became apparent and moved up the snow to join the other on the crest. The first then approached the great rock-step and shortly emerged at the top; the second did likewise. Then the whole fascinating vision vanished, enveloped in cloud once more."

It could be none other than Mallory and

Irvine, and it appeared to him, even at such a great distance, that they were moving "with considerable alacrity." What shocked Odell was that they had still a considerable distance ahead of them and were several hours behind Mallory's professed schedule. It made him anxious, although he felt Mallory and Irvine could still make the summit and retreat safely. What could have happened to make them so late? The ridge route was thought to be quite straightforward, so the pair had met unforeseen difficulties, he surmised. Or had something else delayed the climbers? A snow squall more severe than those earlier in the day caught Odell just as he reached Camp VI a little over an hour later; he was glad to be able to duck inside the tiny mountain tent.

The chaos of strewn belongings, oxygen cylinders, and discarded parts of carrying frames inside Mallory and Irvine's tent has been interpreted as evidence of a last minute problem with the oxygen apparatus that Irvine was desperately trying to fix, delaying their departure. This is as likely a scenario as any, although it is not one Odell particularly subscribed to; he did once say that there were so many bits and pieces of the apparatus at the camp that he could not be certain they had taken any oxygen sets with them at all that day. But he also wrote in the expedition book that Irvine was an inveterate tinkerer. "He loved to dwell amongst, nay, reveled in, pieces of apparatus and a litter of tools, and was never happier than when up against some mechanical difficulty!" At 27,000 feet, and in the dark, however, it seems unlikely that Irvine busied himself with any unnecessary tinkering.

The snow did not let up, and after a while Odell decided to go a bit higher to see if he could spot the pair. The weather might have induced them to turn round, he thought, and in the mist he could imagine it might be difficult to find their tent, tucked in its alcove of rock. He struck out across the mountainside in the direction of the summit, whistling and yodeling in the hope they might hear him. The wind had a sharp, cold edge now, at times forcing Odell to seek shelter from the sleety blast behind a rock. After an hour he decided to return to the haven of Camp VI. He was doing no good here; Mallory and Irvine had to be well out of earshot, even if they were returning. They might even be above the blizzard. As he regained the tent, the squall blew over and the whole mountain was washed in sunshine. The fresh snow quickly began to evaporate. Odell scanned the upper crags for another glimpse of his friends. But there was nothing.

Mallory had warned Odell to be sure to get back to Camp IV that evening, maybe even to evacuate it and go lower. Clearly, he had in mind the long and rapid descent Finch and Bruce had made in 1922, all the way down to Camp III after their high climb, and was hoping that he and Irvine might follow their example. It was 4:30 p.m. already, and to Odell it seemed unlikely that the pair would get far this day; there certainly wouldn't be room for three in this little tent. He needed to get down and make space for them. Leaving Mallory's compass, which he had retrieved from Camp V, just inside the door, Odell closed up the tent and made his way down the crest of the north ridge. He kept looking back up the mountain, but could see no sign of the others. There was no point in making the diversion to Camp V on the eastern side of the ridge, and he kept going. The snow was hard and steep in places, and he was able to speed his descent with some standing glissades, which brought him back into Camp IV by 6:45 p.m. There, Hazard plied him with "amazing quantities" of tea and soup to rehydrate him after his two days of high-altitude effort.

The evening was clear, with a bright moon. He and Hazard watched the upper slopes until late at night, hoping for signs that Mallory and Irvine had returned to their tent. The camp was just visible from the Col. But they saw no lights on the mountain, no torches, no flares. Nothing.

Odell had managed to remain optimistic throughout the day and evening of the 8th; it had been such a period of intense experiences for him—as he said, "alike romantic, aesthetic and scientific"—that he was still transfigured at the recollection of it all, and he still harbored the expectancy that "the resolute pair...might at any instant appear returning with news of final conquest." By the next morning when there were still no signs of movement as they scrutinized the upper camp through their field-glasses, a sick feeling of dread began to build within Odell. By noon, he could bear the inactivity and suspense no longer. Hazard could not be persuaded to accompany him, but two sherpas rather reluctantly agreed to set off once more for the high camps.

The bitter cross wind that was so much a feature of this part of the route blew more strongly than the last time Odell had climbed to Camp V. Nonetheless he made good progress, reaching the camp at about 3:30 p.m. He didn't have sufficient time to make Camp VI in daylight; he'd sleep at V and continue in the morning. It was a blustery, cold night, and the little tents seemed ready to be torn from their inadequate roots and hurled down the mountainside. Odell added more rocks to the guy lines of his and his porters' tents.

He knew beyond a shadow of doubt that the prospects for his friends were as bleak as they could be. Even inside the tent, taking advantage of two sleeping bags, Odell could not stay warm, nor could he sleep for his agitation. The porters had fared no better, and the next morning he packed a few things in a rucksack to go down and scribbled some lines to Hazard: "There seems no particular advantage in getting, or trying to get, either of these coolies to come on with me, so I am sending them down with this note." He would proceed alone to Camp VI, but expected to return to Camp IV later that night. The two had prearranged an elaborate code of signals in the form of blankets laid out on a convenient patch of snow, visible from one camp to another. "Don't be certain of seeing signals from VI," Odell now warned Hazard, "but be on the lookout after 11:30, when I shall probably reach there....Too boisterous last night to signal with fleabags. There's nothing to report."

This time Odell took an oxygen set with him. It was one he'd found dumped on the slope two days previously and carried up to Camp V, where he'd found it leaked badly. It was probably known to have been faulty as Irvine had cannibalized the mouthpiece. Odell had brought a spare part with him this time. Even so, he found he derived little benefit from it. He turned up the flow rate. "Perhaps it just allayed a trifle the tire in one's legs," Odell allowed, but not sufficiently to make a convert of him. And the rubber mouthpiece was "objectionable." He turned off the set and experienced none of the feelings of collapse and breathing difficulties the doomsayers had predicted. He did not dump the apparatus but carried it with him against emergencies. "I seemed to get on quite as well," he would recall afterward, while admitting "the hard breathing at these altitudes would surprise even a long-distance runner."

At Camp VI, nothing had changed. No-one had been there. A tent pole had collapsed, that was all. No hope, then. His worst fears realized. Sloughing off the oxygen set, with some relief, he immediately went in search of the missing men: "This upper part of Everest must be indeed the remotest and least hospitable spot on earth, but at no time more emphatically and impressively so than when a darkened atmosphere hides its features and a gale races over its cruel face. And how and when more cruel could it ever seem than when balking one's every step to find one's friends?"

But what hope was there on such a vast and broken mountainside. As he said, "Weeks of diligent search by a party fully equipped for such difficult and particularly trying work at that altitude might not produce any result or

Approaching Camp IV, expedition members and porters are mere ants on a sugary landscape.

unravel the mystery."

The bitter west wind blew forcefully all day, "blowing snow and mist and stuff." Visibility was very poor. After scrambling about on the slabs to the west of Camp VI, up to a height Odell supposed to approach 28,000 feet, he came miserably back to the tent and pulled out the sleeping bags. Dragging them up steep rocks behind the camp where there was a patch of snow on top, he took advantage of a lull in the wind to lay the bags out in the form of a "T," the signal for "No trace can be found; given up hope." Four thousand feet below Hazard picked up the signal, and the sad news was relayed down to advance base camp with more bags in the form of a cross.

From the tent, Odell retrieved Mallory's compass and an oxygen set as modified to Irvine's design, the only items it seemed to him worth bringing down. Anxious as he was to get off the mountain now, cruel as he found it, having consumed his two best friends, he confessed afterward to still feeling the allure of its towering presence. It was almost an enchantment, and he could imagine Mallory and Irvine succumbing to it. No mountaineer could but be fascinated, he said. "He who approaches close must ever be led on, and oblivious of all obstacles seek to reach that most sacred and highest place of all."

It required a conscious suppression of desire, to muster the will for downward flight. But once on his way, the buffeting winds and sleety blasts demanded his complete attention as he negotiated the exposed and awkward slabs, lethal now under wet ice and snow. From time to time he was forced to cower in the lee of rocks to escape the teeth of the wind and to reassure himself that he was not developing symptoms of frostbite. Hazard saw him coming down and sent out Nima to meet him, the last porter remaining on the col. Odell was relieved to learn that Norton had instructed that no further searches should be made, and that everyone was to come off the mountain.

Andrew Irvine's rope ladder made it much easier for porters to haul loads of equipment and supplies onto the North Col.

The period of waiting for news in the lower camps had seemed interminable. Norton said they passed through "every successive stage of suspense and anxiety from high hope to hopelessness. Even when, inwardly, everyone knew there was no hope, they could not relinquish its last stirrings without firm news." Somervell's diary on June 10 recorded: "No news as yet—but weather is not too bad, and it may be that they have done it. We ought to hear tomorrow." But on the 11th, the entry reads: "No news. It is ominous. A few people have filtered back to the Base, very pessimistic. It is very disappointing to think that Mallory and Irvine may have failed—but they may never come back. They may be dead. My friend and fellow-climber, Mallory, one in spirit with me—dead? I can hardly believe it."

Captain Noel, at Camp III, described how hope faded by the hour. "Norton," he said, "paced backwards and forwards in front of his tent, speaking little, visibly affected and, I think, already resigned to the worst. Hingston had all his medical aids ready and was prepared to go out at once in answer to a call from the support party up the mountain." Noel had left his rocky

Looking backward, a 1922 panorama captures the scene on the North Col that greeted the expedition two years later. In the far distance at right, slung between two low peaks, is Lhakpa La, the pass from which Mallory first sighted the North Col and its approaches.

eyrie on the cliff behind camp and set up his telescope close to the mess tent. His photographic assistants took turns at keeping watch through it, and he periodically peered through it himself to make sure they were missing nothing. Banks of cloud were building up beyond the Rapiu La, indicating that the monsoon had reached Bengal and would soon be upon them.

Suddenly, the watchers shouted that there was activity on the Col. Figures came to the edge of the ice shelf to make the blanket signal. "As we watched we again hoped against hope, that they would tell us they had found them, frostbitten—exhausted—incapable of moving—anything, but still alive. While life existed we could go to the rescue and do our best and utmost...." But, it was not to be. The signal spelled "Death." Noel filmed the blanket cross.

"What is it? What do you see?" Geoffrey Bruce wanted to know. Wordlessly, Noel passed the telescope to him so that he might see for himself.

Norton called an impromptu conference. Pointing out that any further search was as futile as it was dangerous, he told the others that the criterium now should be to get Odell, Hazard, and Nima down safely. There was no dissent. Hingston went out on the glacier and placed three blankets evenly apart. Those on the Col would know this read: "Abandon search. Return as soon as possible with party."

The blanket code had been devised within the expedition to cope with the emergency situation. Another code had been worked out

before the expedition left England so that *The Times* could receive expedition news ahead of dispatches and ahead of its rivals. Accordingly, Norton sent the following coded telegram from base camp the next day: OBTERRAS LONDON—MALLORY IRVINE NOVE REMAINDER ALCEDO—NORTON RONGBUK. Then he began the painful business of composing a dispatch to send home, advising of the tragic deaths.

On the morning of the 11th, the three men on the Col packed up what they could, left the tents standing, and with heavy loads descended the slopes by the 1922 avalanche route in half an hour. They were soon back with their friends at Camp III. After "tiffin," Hingston and Shebbeare struck this camp too, and the retreat began.

"We were a sad little party," Norton wrote of this period afterward. "From the first we accepted the loss of our comrades in that rational spirit which all of our generation had learnt in the Great War, and there was never a tendency to a morbid harping on the irrevocable. But the tragedy was very near; our friends' vacant tents and vacant places at table were a constant reminder to us of what the atmosphere of the camp would have been had things gone differently."

Odell was surprised to discover how much weight he has lost; he was glad to be down. "Glorious glacier walk," he records that day, the 11th, and the next, "glorious walk down good moraine track" to Base. He had enough energy in reserve to investigate the strange Earth towers on the way in the Main Rongbuk Valley, and he was delighted to see so many alpine flowers making their appearance. The 13th brought him his first bath for a month, and he treated himself to a restful day, sorting

out his geological specimens and packing up and labeling Mallory's and Irvine's kit for the homeward journey, while Somervell and Beetham organized the construction of a memorial cairn, bearing the names of the 12 dead of three expeditions. After supper on Saturday the 14th, they had a big bonfire of all the old boxes that were not going home, and Captain Noel completed his photographic "offensive" by taking photographs of all surviving team members.

Hingston had already given every climber a medical examination. Without exception, all who had been to the Col or above had dilated hearts to some degree, although this was expected to be only a temporary condition. Odell who had climbed up and down more than anyone and had, with the exception of one night, spent 12 consecutive nights above 23,000 feet, was the one who suffered least. They were all wasted, with an assortment of coughs, stripped throats and frostbites. Norton proposed to take the

Dear Noel
We'll probably start
early to-morrow (8th) in order
to have clear weather. It
won't be too early to start
looking out for us either
crossing the rock band under
the pyramid or going up skyline
at 8.0 p.m.

Yours ever
G Mallory

When Odell photographed Mallory (left) and Irvine before leaving the North Col for their attempt at Everest's summit, little did he know he was taking the last picture of the pair alive. Two days later, at Camp VI, Mallory had written a note for cinematographer John Noel, hoping he might catch a glimpse of them on their final approach:

> *Dear Noel,*
>
> *We'll probably start early to-morrow (8th) in order to have clear weather. It won't be too early to start looking out for us either crossing the rock band under the pyramid or going up skyline at 8.0 p.m.*
>
> *Yours ever*
>
> *G Mallory*

Mallory clearly meant 8:00 a.m. in his final sentence.

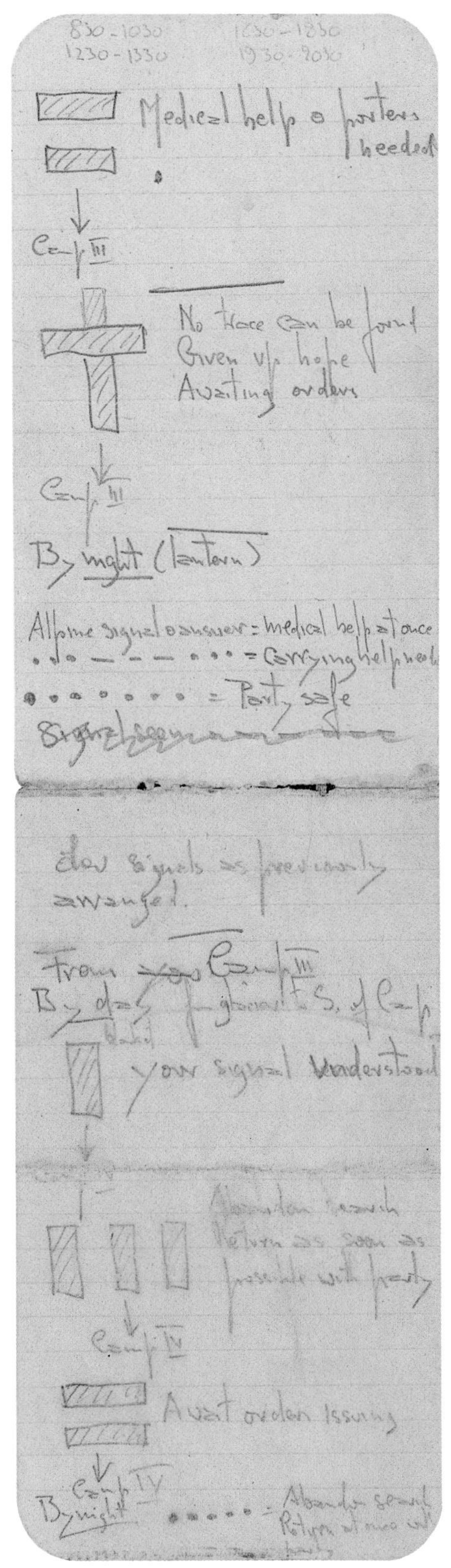
830-1030 1230-1330
1630-1830 1930-2030
Medical help & porters needed
Camp III
No trace can be found
Given up hope
Awaiting orders
Camp III
By night (lantern)
Party safe
Other signals as previously arranged.
From Camp III
Your signal understood
Abandon search
Return as soon as possible with party
Camp IV
Await orders issuing
Camp IV
By night
Abandon search

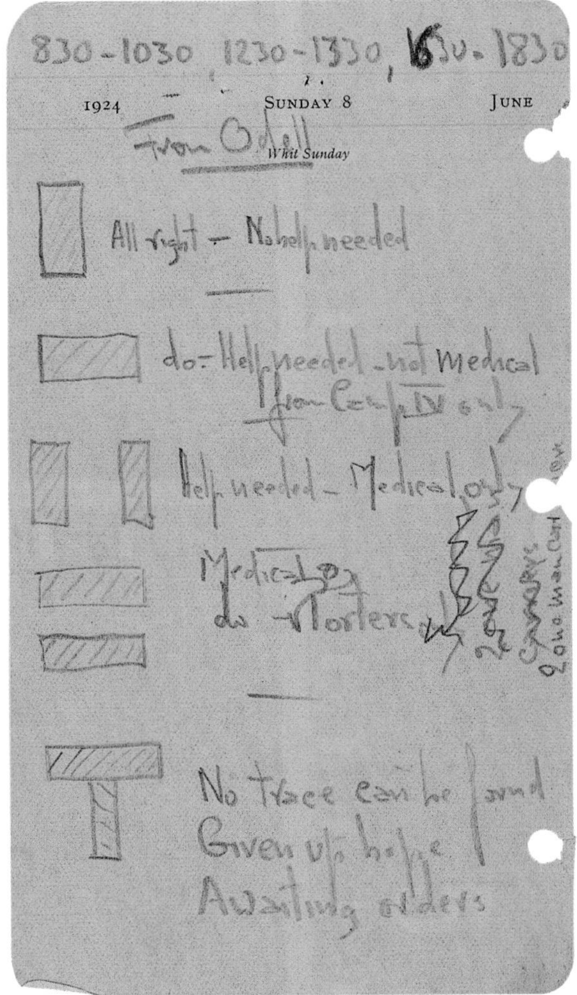
830-1030, 1230-1330, 1630-1830
1924 SUNDAY 8 JUNE
Whit Sunday
From Odell
All right – No help needed
do – Help needed – not medical from Camp IV only
Help needed – Medical only
Medical do – Porters
No trace can be found
Given up hope
Awaiting orders

On separate sheets of paper, Hazard worked out a code for transmitting information about the fates of Mallory and Irvine. Possible messages ranged from an all's well to a call for medical aid to a sad resignation that the worst had occurred. Twice Odell launched one-man search parties from North Col, without success. Finally, when he was confident there was no hope, he lay two sleeping bags in a "T," the agreed-upon signal that the pair were presumed dead.

Four thousand feet below, Hazard in turn positioned six blankets in the shape of a large cross, in view of observers below in Advance Base Camp.

Norton replied with three blankets, "Abandon search. Return as soon as possible with party."

main party to the unknown Rongshar Valley under Guarisankar for ten days' recuperation at low altitudes before the long march back to Darjeeling. Captain Noel, however, would return at once, accompanying the porters and loads. Hazard, too, ducked out of the side trip; he wanted to complete the survey of the West Rongbuk with Hari Sing Thapa of the Indian Survey, the unfinished portion of the 1921 map. They bade farewell to the venerable Rongbuk Lama on 16th June. The long-expected monsoon had still not reached Everest.

On the way back Odell had a detour of his own he wished to make. Norton agreed he could go if he took Shebbeare with him, who knew some Tibetan. Odell's geological ardor was treated as a bit of a joke among his colleagues, and before they left the main party, Geoffrey Bruce drew Shebbeare to one side and prophesied that once this trip was over, he wouldn't want to set eyes on Odell again. "At the time I thought he was probably right," Shebbeare wrote later in his diary, "for Odell, a wonder on a mountain, is quite useless in the ordinary affairs of life and, knowing no oriental language, was not likely to be much help on adventure of this sort.

"Nevertheless, the prophecy proved quite wrong; it had failed to take into account one golden quality that Odell possessed, that of never worrying himself or anybody else. In an emergency, and we had plenty of emergencies on our trip, he never offered fatuous advice. Instead, he would sit placidly on a rock and read *The Times Literary Supplement,* a copy of which, by that time many months old, he always carried in his rucksack, and so he would wait for the situation to clear. It made you ashamed to worry and at the same time heartened you to get something done to justify such implicit confidence. So far from never wanting to see him again, we had no sooner rejoined the main body than we got permission to leave it again and, two marches later, we were off on our own once more, cutting down through Sikkim and did not see the rest of them again until we all met in Darjeeling."

Norton's coded cable, which had left Base Camp by runner on June 11, was telegraphed from Phari Dzong and arrived in London on June 19. Ruth Mallory, in Cambridge, learned of her husband's death from a member of the press before the news broke in the newspapers on the 21st. Stunned, she went out for a long walk with friends.

The level of public interest in the tragedy took almost everyone by surprise. Ruth was touched by the number of letters and messages she received, as were the parents of both George and Sandy. The Everest Committee fielded all the formal letters of condolence from foreign Alpine Clubs and dignitaries, and the King George sent a telegram to Sir Francis Younghusband, saying, "They will ever be remembered as fine examples of mountaineers—ready to risk their lives for their companions and to face dangers on behalf of science and discovery."

Among the letters Ruth treasured was that written by Norton a few days after George's disappearance in an endeavor to bring her some

The ridge along which Noel hoped to spot Mallory and Irvine with his movie camera was not visible from Advance Base Camp. Cinematographer John Noel had to haul his equipment another 800 feet up to his "Eagle's Nest" in order to get a good view (top).

Filming from the Advance Base Camp on June 10, Noel filmed the dejected party on North Col walking away from their cross of blankets.

comfort in her grief. "Everything points to the probability of a sudden death," he tells her, "a slip by one or the other—a purely mountaineering accident. It is hard to invent any hypothesis which will cover the facts entailing the idea of a lingering death from exposure, nor is there any reason to suppose that any defect in the oxygen apparatus could have been the cause."

"We were a sad little party," said Norton (second from left, seated) of his fellow survivors of the 1924 Mount Everest Expedition, who posed for one last portrait before striking Base Camp. "Vacant tents and vacant places at table were a constant reminder to us of what the atmosphere of the camp would have been had things gone differently."

Norton always felt, he said, that he'd usurped the position Mallory would have filled had he not joined the expedition at the last minute. Conscious of his "inferior qualifications" for the role of climbing leader, he was grateful to George for backing him through thick and thin. "His bottomless capacity for work and his determination to win were my prop and stay," he told her. This great mountaineer and "gallant, gentle soul" compelled the admiration of all his colleagues and was at the same time a real "pal" to all. "You can't share a 16 lb high-altitude tent for days and weeks with a man under conditions of some hardship without getting to know his innermost soul," Norton said, "and I think I know almost as you do what his was made of—pure gold."

Geoffrey Young, too, took Mallory's death hard, especially coming so soon after the Mallory's had moved to Cambridge and become neighbors. He was in France when the news broke, and he wrote to Ruth on June 30, "Until we knew more I could not write. And I really can't now: it is a long numbness of pain, and yet but a shadow of yours, for indeed one cannot think of you separately. An unspeakable pride in that magnificent courage and endurance, that joyous and supreme triumph of human spirit over all circumstances, all mortal resistance; and the loss unutterable... ." During the next month, with no lessening in his sense of loss, Young wrote to George Trevelyan, another old friend and Pen-y-Pass habitué: "And so here I am in middle life, with not one left of my alpine companions and pupils... . Just memories. I am thinking of George Mallory and the last venture, day and night. So fatally unnecessary—but a fate has dogged the leadership on Everest. In every year the leadership has lapsed to him, without the responsibility that might have steadied his judgement into a cooler detachment. In weighing the balance, I attach no glamour or importance to the circumstance of his death; it was as accidental a consequence as his choice of life, and of his temperament, as my losing my leg. It was his life was important... ."

For a long time after she received the news, Ruth found part of herself still clung to the hope that it might after all be a ghastly mistake, an error in transmission, perhaps; that when the team sailed home, there George would be, smiling, among his companions. Coming to terms with her loss would be so much easier, she felt, if she could know whether "it was his time." She placed great store by this, telling Geoffrey Young , that it was not difficult for

her to believe George's spirit was ready for another life, and his way of going to it was very beautiful. What grieved her almost beyond enduring was that their three small children would never know the extent of their loss. She attended to all the necessary formalities of death and comforted George's parents, while all the time keeping her own feelings tightly under control. Never one to be openly demonstrative, she now appeared to her volatile mother-in-law as "almost too stoical"—"She reminds me of a stately lily with its head broken and hanging down," George's mother said.

Ruth opened up only to Young. Through him she felt closest to George. "I do not think this pain matters at all," she told him, in one of several letters that have survived from this period. "I know George did not mean to be killed; he meant not to be so hard that I did not a bit think he would be... . I don't think I do feel that his death makes me the least more proud of him, it is his life that I loved and love. I know so absolutely that he could not have failed in courage or self-sacrifice. Whether he got to the top of the mountain or did not, whether he lived or died, makes no difference to my admiration for him. I think I have got the pain separate. There is so much of it, and it will go on so long, that I must do that... . Oh, Geoffrey, if only it hadn't happened! It so easily might not have."

GEORGE LEIGH MALLORY, 1886-1924

CHAPTER SEVEN

Together these two went up the mountain for the last time:
higher than ever man has been before they were last seen—
one giving a hand to the other, and then—they were seen no more.
Could either have wished for a better friend to hold his hand
at the crossing into the unknown land beyond?

LT. COL. E. F. NORTON, OCTOBER 1924

INTO LEGEND

"Poor Mr and Mrs Irvine...are terribly broken down," Mallory's mother wrote to one of her daughters on June 22. "I don't think they had in the least realized how great the risk was."

Sandy Irvine was given two terms' leave of absence from Merton College, Oxford, for the Everest trip. The college, like his parents, would have seen it as an honor for him to be chosen to represent his country, and a great opportunity. This may have outweighed other concerns about his participation. It is certain his death brought deep grief to all who knew him; Irvine's father we know never got over the loss.

Fourteen years younger than the average age of the party (sixteen years younger than Mallory), "our blue-eyed boy from Oxford is...a really good sort," Somervell had written. "Neither bumptious by virtue of his 'blue', nor squashed by the age of the rest of us. Mild, but strong, full of common sense, good at gadgets....Thoroughly a man (or boy) of the world, yet with high ideals. And, he is very decent with the porters."

It's hard to guess whether being so much younger than the other climbers isolated Irvine. Perhaps there were times—when his colleagues were swapping war stories or reliving old climbing triumphs—when to share a laugh with someone his own age would have been a comfort. Odell has commented that toward the end of the expedition Sandy became more withdrawn. One wonders if Irvine's general helpfulness was merely the expression of good nature on his part—for it surely went beyond his duties as Mess Secretary—or if it was the easiest way to bridge the gap with his older companions? Contemporaries have testified to Irvine's shyness, saying it was not always easy to pass beyond the barriers of his reserve. But his modest assurance endeared him to everyone.

"From the word go," Norton told Sandy's parents in a letter of condolence written within days of his disappearance, "he was a complete and absolute success in every way. He was spoken of by General Bruce in an early communiqué as our 'experiment.' I can assure you that his experimental stage was a short one as he almost at once became almost indispensable. It was not only that we leant on him for every conceivable mechanical requirement—it was more that we found we could trust his capacity, ingenuity and astonishingly ready good nature to be equal to any call....He took his place automatically without a hint of the gaucherie of youth, from the very start, as one of the most popular members of our mess."

His splendid strength was manifest, Norton said, on those occasions when he carried for faltering porters "heavier loads than any European had ever carried before." He recalled how, with Somervell, Irvine hauled a dozen porters' loads up a 150-foot ice cliff on the way to the North Col. "I can hardly bear to think of him now as I last saw him on the North Col."

Among the several memorial services that autumn for Mallory and Irvine was one held at St. Paul's Cathedral in London on October 17. The eulogy was delivered by the Bishop of Chester. "It is not for us timid pedestrians to pretend that we understand your love of the heights," he said. But having learned something of the boyhood and early years of these two Cheshire men, the bishop had come to believe that set in their hearts was more than the love of high mountains. Allied to this was the ascent of spiritual altitudes, splendid peaks of courage and unselfishness and cheerfulness such as are reached not necessarily by the sure-footed and the clearheaded but always by the compassionate, the brotherly, and the pure in heart. Concluding, he adapted the lament of King David, "Delightful and very pleasant were George Mallory and Andrew Irvine; in life, in death, they were not parted."

That same evening the Royal Geographical Society and the Alpine Club held their joint meeting "to Receive the Reports from the Mount Everest Expedition of 1924." Such was the popular interest that the Committee had to use the Royal Albert Hall for the occasion. The program concluded with a description by Odell of his support mission, dramatic sighting, and his forlorn search for his friends. "The question remains," he said. "Has Mount Everest been climbed? It must be left unanswered, for

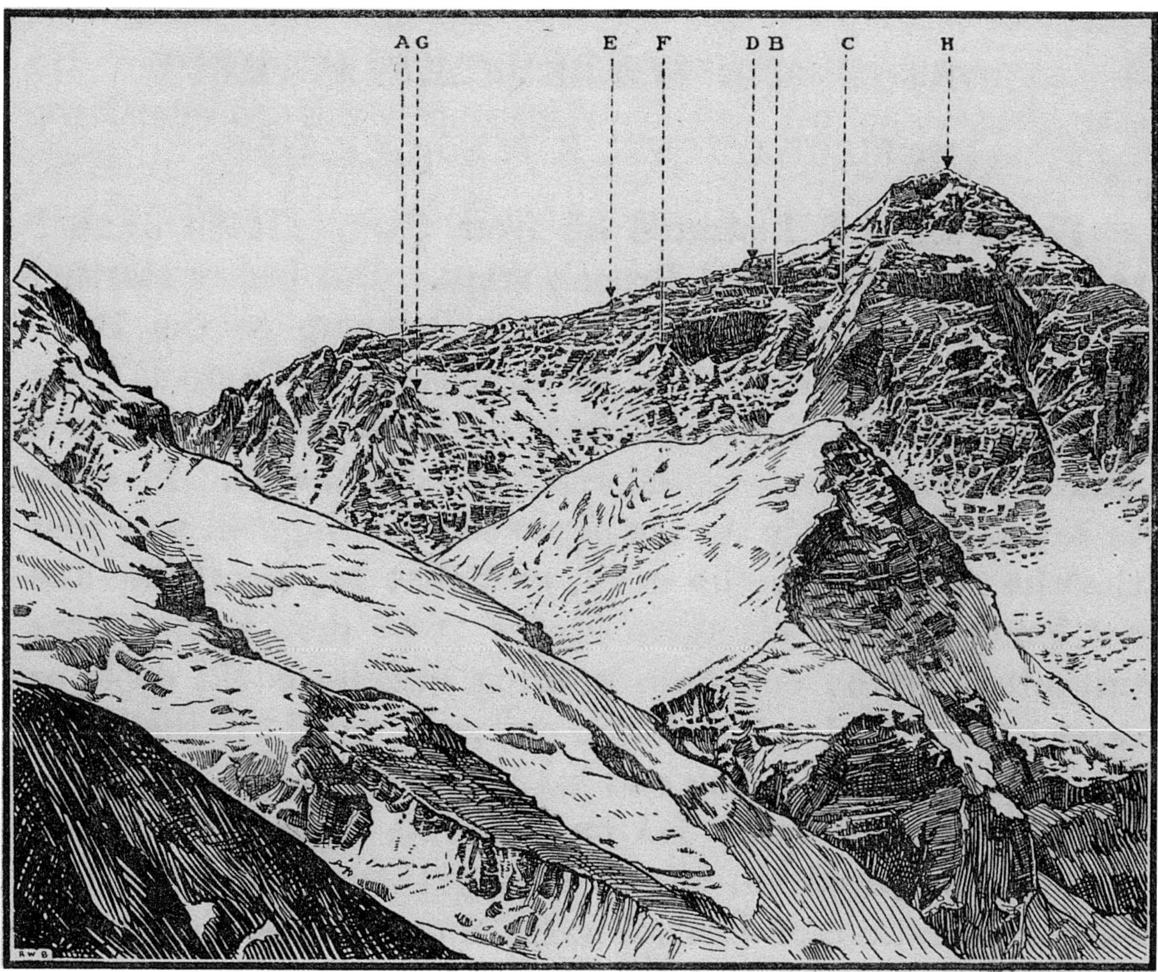

there is no direct evidence. But bearing in mind all the circumstances...and considering their position when last seen, I think there is a strong probability that Mallory and Irvine succeeded. At that I must leave it."

Though many of his fellows shared his belief, and all strongly hoped it was true that the summit had been reached before the pair died, Odell was alone in believing they died of exposure. Norton had written from Base Camp that he was "very sorry Odell put that bit about their dying of exposure in his communiqué,"

Early published reports of the expedition, such as this one from 1925, clearly indicated that Mallory and Irvine had at least made it past the Second Step. It was the most optimistic interpretation of Odell's last misty sightings of the pair.
Key:
A. Camp VI, 26,700 feet
B. The point reached by Somervell in 1924
C. The point reached by Norton in 1924
D. "The Second Step," where Mallory and Irvine were last seen
E. "The First Step"
F. The point reached by Finch and Geoffrey Bruce in 1922
G. The point reached by Mallory, Norton, and Somervell in 1922
H. The summit, 29,002 feet

telling the Committee: "All the rest of us are agreed that it is any odds on a fall-off."

But both Norton and Odell, speaking or writing of Mallory afterward, chose their words with great care. While stressing how ardently Mallory desired the summit and how much he felt its deadly attraction, neither believed he would ever have risked the life of his young companion. However near the summit they were, he would have turned back in good time to ensure a safe return. Yet other Edwardian romantics saw nothing wrong in a willing sacrifice for a mountain. And certainly not this mountain of mountains. Younghusband, for one, would think it a virtue not to turn back with the prize so close. "Say he was actually on the final pyramid; say he was only a couple of hundred feet in height, and less than two hundred yards in distance from the summit, and that his watch showed him that it was four o'clock; would he forthwith put it back in his pocket and turn his steps downward? And even if he himself had that superhuman self-control would his younger companion have the same? Wouldn't Irvine have said: 'I don't care what happens. I'm going to have my fling for the top.' And could Mallory have held out any longer? Wouldn't he rather have given in with joyous relief?"

Longstaff felt so. "It's obvious to any climber that they got up," he said. "You cannot expect of that pair to weigh the chances of return—I should be weighing them still—it

Before the team began the arduous return march across the Tibetan Plateau to Darjeeling, they descended to the forests and moist, thick air of the Rongshar Valley where Col. Norton painted this watercolor of Guarisankar on June 26, 1924.

sounds a fair day: probably they were above those clouds that hid them from Odell; how they must have appreciated that view of half the world; it was worthwhile to them; now they'll never grow old and I am very sure they would not change places with any of us."

Geoffrey Young, with nearly 20 years knowledge of Mallory as a mountaineer, was convinced they made the top."Difficult as it would have been for any mountaineer to turn back with the only difficulty past—to Mallory it would have been an impossibility," he declared. His eloquent tributes to his friend did much to color the way Mallory is remembered. But privately, as Young mourned the loss of a friend, he was not so sure this particular challenge should have been taken up at all—certainly not by Mallory, whom he had urged not to go to Everest again. Many years later, he would tell an acquaintance that he thought young Sandy Irvine "a very fine type. But Mallory should not have taken him on that lone venture."

Odell's intriguing sighting has been central to all speculation—at the time and since—of what might have happened on that last day on the mountain. And, by its nature as a near-mystical moment granted through the swirling mists of eternity, it also has been an important ingredient in the process of mythologizing Mallory and Irvine through the months and

General Bruce (far right) had to leave the third tragic Everest expedition due to illness, but he rejoined the team upon their return to India. Based on Odell's testimony, he felt sure that the top was reached and that Mallory and Irvine were overtaken on their way back, probably by dark. "Anyhow," he wrote home, "it's dreadful—heartbreaking but wonderful."

years that have followed. It symbolizes so much: the striving of man for the pinnacle between Earth and heaven; braving unknown elemental forces; conquering pain and will; the bond of friendship transcending age, transcending death; the sacrifice; the mystery.

"Brothers till death, and a wind-swept grave, Joy of the journey's ending: Ye who have climbed to the great white veil, Heard ye the chant? Saw ye the Grail?" These Arthurian lines by Geoffrey Young, romanticizing death in high mountains, one could imagine as having been inspired by the affecting loss of Mallory and Irvine. Curiously—prophetically almost—they predate the tragedy by many years, appearing in a collection of poems in 1909, the year Young met the youthful, impressionable Mallory and bestowed upon him the nickname "Galahad" for his pure, questing spirit. It is this questing spirit that Odell's last vision so neatly epitomizes. It is hard to imagine the legend of Mallory and Irvine having the same potency and enduring appeal without this iconic vignette to feed the imagination.

It is hard to extract exactly what Odell experienced in that euphoric moment. Assuming his diary entry for June 8 to be the first expression of his recollection, he has Mallory and Irvine "on ridge nearing base of final pyramid." Once down the mountain, he wrote a dispatch for the *Times* that left Rongbuk Base Camp on June 14. With events still fairly fresh in his mind, he reports that a sudden clearing revealed "the entire summit, ridge, and final peak of Everest." His eyes pick up a "black spot silhouetted on a small snow crest beneath a rock step in the ridge," and he sees this spot move up the snow to join the other on the crest: "The first then approached the great rock step, and shortly emerged at the top. The second did likewise. Then the whole fascinating vision vanished enveloped in cloud once more." And he pinpoints the place on the ridge as "a prominent rock step at a very short distance from the base of the final pyramid."

We can imagine Odell's comrades pressing to know exactly what he means here. Poring over a photograph perhaps, jabbing fingers up and down the picture, or looking up at the distant view of the ridge from Base Camp, they would say to him, "Come on, you must remember. Which "great step" are we talking about?" The next time Odell relates the story, at the Albert Hall meeting, he is saying that, with the whole summit ridge unveiled, he notices "far away on a snow slope leading up to the last step but one from the base of the final pyramide, a tiny object moving...." His first moving "object" climbs to the top of the step, and at that moment mists engulf the picture once more—before the second has a chance to join the first. Although "the last step but one" sounds confusing, we know Odell is referring to what we call now the Second Step, since he makes a point in his notes for this lecture of correcting the false position given by Hinks in the *Geographical Journal*. He is allowing the existence of a third "step," therefore, between the Second Step and the summit—and it's true a minor step-feature does intervene, one of no relevance to climbers as it is easily bypassed, but a knob on the skyline nonetheless. Odell has added more now about the tiny figures he saw, and a degree of speculation:

"They were moving expeditiously as if endeavouring to make up for lost time. True, they were moving one at a time over what was apparently but moderately difficult ground, but one cannot definitely conclude from this that they were roped—an important consideration in any estimate of what befell them. I had seen that there was a considerable quantity of new snow covering some of the upper rocks near the summit ridge and this may well have caused delay in the ascent. Burdened as they undoubtedly were with the oxygen apparatus, these snow-covered, debris sprinkled slabs may have given much trouble. The oxygen apparatus itself may have needed repair or readjustment either before or after thay left Camp VI, or so have delayed them. Or both these factors may have been operative."

By the time the expedition book came out the following year, the consensus of opinion had shifted. The tiny figures were thought to have been on the First, rather than the Second Step. Additionally, some qualifications have crept into Odell's account. He describes at length the relationship between the First and Second steps. Now, when he talks of the "last step but one," we can take it he is referring to the First Step and not the Second. His passage opens with the summit ridge still entirely clear, as before, but contradicts itself a few lines further on when Odell explains that his difficulty in placing the figures precisely on one or other of the larger steps was "owing to the small portion of the summit ridge uncovered." At the time he said he took them to be on the upper of the two steps, now he acknowledges it could have been the lower one. Though this would put another couple of hours between the pair and the summit, he does not alter his conviction that they made it.

Before leaving Base Camp, the expedition members built a pyramidal cairn engraved with the names of all who had died on their treks since 1921. Seven decades later, for whatever reasons, all the stones had been carried away.

While those who knew and loved Mallory clung firmly to the idea that he and Irvine climbed to the summit before they died, many were expressing misgivings over the reliability of Odell's evidence. Longstaff gives the hint when he says in December 1924, "Unless they had been going fast—that is, at an Alpine rate—it's hard to believe that Odell could have seen them at all at that distance." Such doubts would only increase. Indeed, by the time the next expedition went to Everest in 1933, its members were wondering if Odell could have seen any figures at all: wasn't it possible he'd been misled by rocks on a snow slope, which, viewed from about a mile away, only appeared to move? They cited an occasion that year when, close to their Camp VI, Eric Shipton had

IN·MEMORY
OF·THREE·
EVEREST·
EXPEDITIONS.
1921
KELLAS
1922
LHAKPA
NARBU-
PASANG
PEMA
SANGE
TEMBA
1924
MALLORY

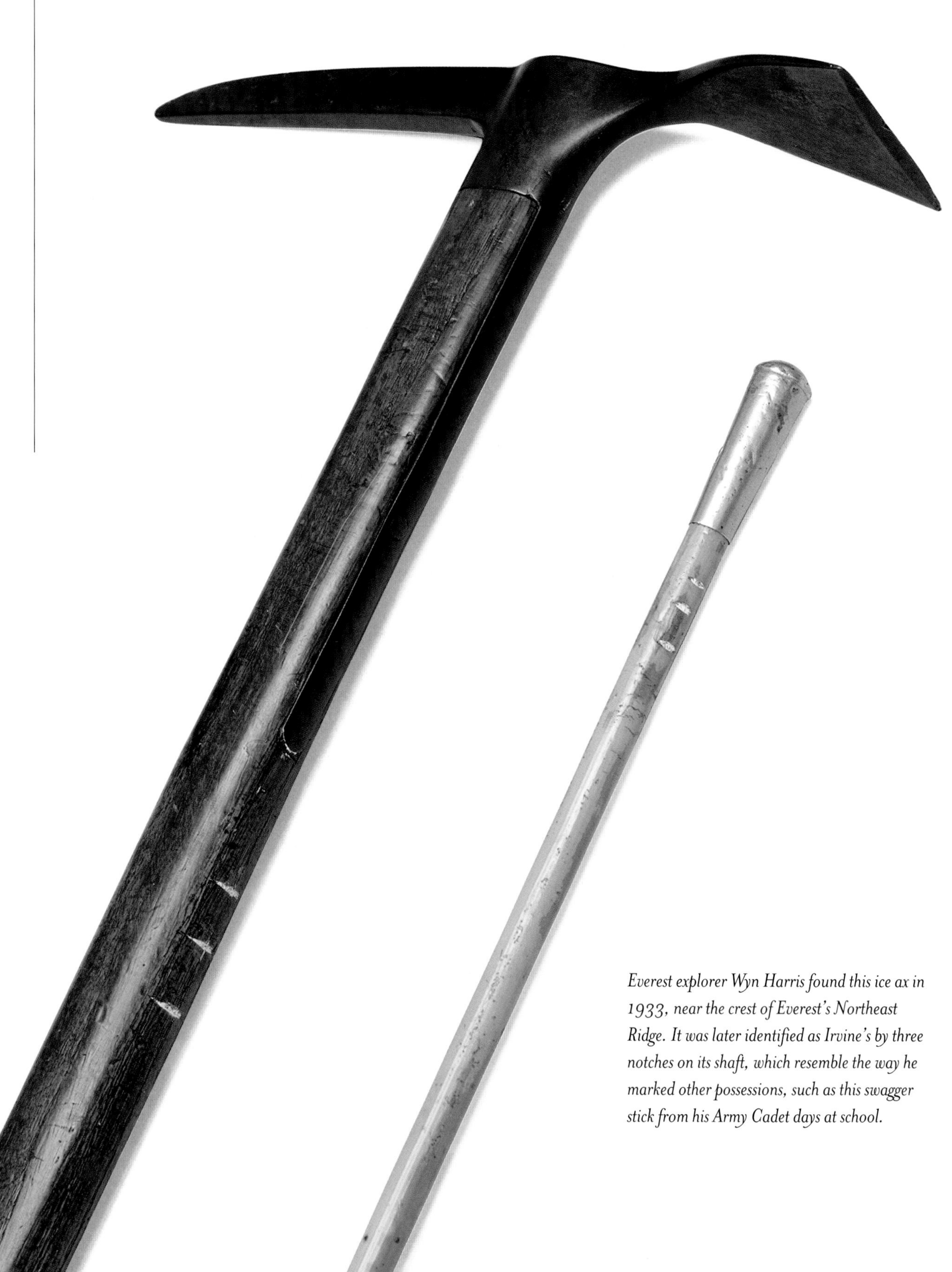

Everest explorer Wyn Harris found this ice ax in 1933, near the crest of Everest's Northeast Ridge. It was later identified as Irvine's by three notches on its shaft, which resemble the way he marked other possessions, such as this swagger stick from his Army Cadet days at school.

suddenly exclaimed: "There go Wyn and Waggers on the Second Step!" Percy Wyn Harris and Lawrence Wager were not on the step, however; the little dots seen on the steep snow at the foot of the cliff had to have been rocks, and there were, strangely enough, another couple of rocks immediately above the step that could give the impression the obstacle had been surmounted. Another theory was that Odell had perhaps caught sight of birds flying, Himalayan choughs, not too far away from him but outlined against the snow slope beyond; or cloud shadows perhaps; or that he'd had an altitude-induced hallucination. Was it just a trick of the eye or brain? Did Odell see anything at all?

Odell was fiercely indignant that anyone should think he'd been deluded. In fact, he retorted, after looking at photographs brought back in 1933, he was reinclined to consider the Second Step as after all the most likely position of his revelation. Odell lived to be 96; he had a distinguished geological career, but for all those years after Everest it seemed all people wanted of him was to hear about the day, when as a young man, he caught his epochal vision. Some of his fellow expeditioners would mutter ungenerously that he became more convinced of what he had seen as the years passed than he was at the time. "At the outset I thought they were at what we called the Second Step," he told us shortly before his death in 1987. "Later I could see it might well have been the First...I've never been clear from that day to this which it was." But he was adamant it was people he had seen. "I had no hallucinations. They were moving, actually, moving figures. My records, my diary, my specimens of geology...are all consistent one with the other, and with what I saw. I tell you they were climbers!"

The 1933 expedition to Everest, led by Hugh Ruttledge, provided the next clue. Wyn Harris and Wager, climbing above that expedition's Camp VI at 27,400 ft (halfway up the steep Yellow Band that constitutes the Northeast Ridge) made a remarkable discovery. At a point estimated as 250 yards east of the First Step and some 60 feet below the crest of the Northeast Ridge, they found an ice ax "lying free on smooth, brown 'boiler-plate' slabs, inclined at an easy angle but steepening considerably just below." It could only have belonged to Mallory or Irvine; no one else had been here before them. What particularly astonished him, Wyn Harris said, "was that the steel of the ax was all absolutely bright and the wood was as if it had been cleaned with sandpaper." On the polished steel head was stamped the name of the maker—Willisch of Täsch, in the Zermatt Valley. "To me," Wyn Harris added, "the ax had only one explanation. It marked the scene of a fall by a climber either from the ridge 60 feet above or from the place where the ax was lying. No climber could possibly have left the ax deliberately at the place where I found it."

On the way back from his summit bid, Wyn Harris retrieved the ax, leaving his own in its place to mark the spot. It was brought home and given to the Alpine Club, where for years it was known as "Mallory's ax" and bore a small brass label to that effect. Some time later, from the evidence of three small notches on its shaft,

THE VEST-POCKET CAMERA

BY GRAHAM HOYLAND

When I was a very small boy my father told me about a climbing hero in our family, a man who had been near the summit of Mount Everest in 1924 and who had been a close friend of George Mallory, with whom he shared a tent on Everest.

Years later, when I was 12 and he was 79, I met my great-uncle. I remember standing on the lawn and looking up in awe at the legendary Howard Somervell. He was an extraordinarily gifted man; a climber, a painter, and a doctor. I was transfixed by the incredible story he told me.

On the 1924 expedition, during the rescue of four marooned Sherpas, Somervell's throat was badly frostbitten. Later on, in an oxygen-free summit attempt, he and Col. E. F. Norton reached more than 28,000 feet, higher than any man had been before but still 900 feet from the top. On the way up Somervell took several remarkable photographs using his small folding camera. On their retreat he suddenly started suffocating from an obstruction in his throat. The mucous membrane of his frostbitten larynx had sloughed, blocking his windpipe. Somervell sat down to die, but with a last attempt to clear the blockage he pressed his chest with both hands–and here the old man pushed his chest hard to demonstrate the maneuver to his fascinated audience–and coughed up the mucous membrane. "What a relief! Coughing up a little blood, I once more breathed...freely–more freely than I had for days." Norton and Somervell returned to the North Col and met Mallory and Irvine who were heading up for their last attempt. Mallory had forgotten his camera, and Somervell handed him his Vestpocket Kodak. The two parties separated the next morning, and Somervell never saw his friend Mallory again.

This story spurred me on a lifelong quest. I had to climb Mount Everest for myself, and I had to try to find my great-uncle's camera and learn what secrets it contained. If it could be retrieved, it's thought that a printable photograph might be developed from the decades-old film. At the highest altitudes on Mount Everest, the air is bone-dry and the temperature so low that camera film would be permanently frozen—and, the theory goes, perfectly preserved. A photograph might help solve the mystery of what happened on that June day so many years ago. There was no camera found left behind in Mallory and Irvine's high camp; we assume they carried it with them on their last climb. Mallory was no fool. An Everest summit would be his chance for everlasting glory, and he realized the importance of a summit picture in documenting his success on the mountain.

I have a Vestpocket Kodak identical to the one given to George Mallory by my great-uncle. It's not much larger or heavier than a tin of sardines, and it slips easily into a shirt pocket. But it is not easy to use. To take a picture, you have to unfold the camera and pull out the bellows. Then, instead of looking through a viewfinder, you have to hold the camera at chest level and peer down at a tiny prism. The image reflected in the prism is reversed. You then have to press a small lever and trip the shutter. Imagine doing all this at 28,000 feet, and with numb fingers! No wonder Somervell said he had to make three attempts before he got one usable photograph.

It is a long shot, but there is a chance–just a chance–that lying up there in the eternal snows of Mount Everest is a small tin camera containing a photograph that will shake the mountaineering world and change history. It only remains for someone to go and pick it up.

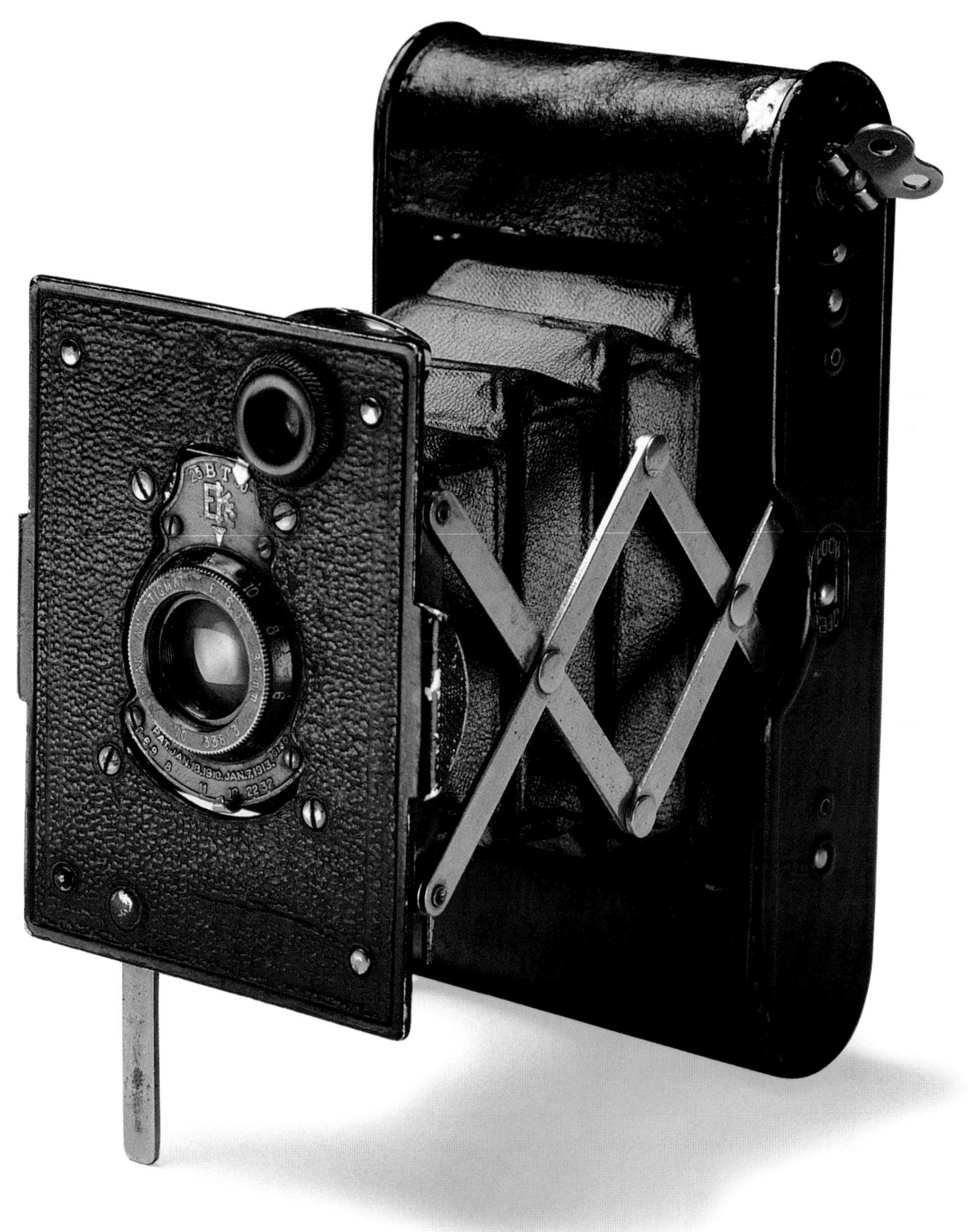

A VESTPOCKET KODAK

While a student at Oxford's Merton College, Andrew Irvine became hooked on mountaineering. He participated in an arctic expedition to eastern Spitsbergen—led by his future Everest colleague Noel Odell. As Irvine's name, linked with Mallory's, made him a national hero, the school dedicated a memorial to him.

which Odell pointed out were almost identical to markings used by Sandy Irvine for identifying some of his belongings, the attribution was revised. The brass label was taken off, turned over, reengraved—henceforth this became "Irvine's ice ax".

This ax was an exciting clue, but what did it mean? Did it indeed mark the scene of an accident? Surely this "easy-angled" ground could not be where Mallory and Irvine met their fate. Yet Wyn Harris was right, it seems inconceivable that an ax would have been abandoned deliberately, however little snow there was on the North Face that year. There may be times on a rock peak in the Alps when you might set down an ax to be collected on the way back, but not here, not on this sloping ground, in this thin air, where it becomes both a walking stick and something to lean over when gasping for breath. As the 1933 climbers pointed out, on Everest as on the Earth's other high mountains, an ax is the climber's best friend and greatest safeguard: "He uses it to help his balance on the outward-dipping slabs, to anchor himself when the treacherous gusts are tearing at his legs, to clear a foothold on the snow-covered rocks and, on occasion, to cut steps across hard patches of snow."

If it had been left behind accidentally, after changing oxygen bottles perhaps, it would not remain lost for long. You'd not go many steps without realizing your "best friend" was absent. If it had been dropped accidentally from above, from the ridge, Wyn Harris was certain it would have been a simple matter to retrieve it. And it was improbable it could have blown there from somewhere nearer the summit. There was no doubt among the climbers that year that this shiny-bright ax on this innocuous-looking ground must indeed mark where the two men fell. Frank Smythe, a member of the 1933 team, supplied a possible scenario in his 1937 book *Camp Six*. He felt that the easiness of the terrain pointed to a slip on the way up rather than down: the heavy oxygen apparatus on the climbers' backs would make a self-arrest almost impossible, he said. Assuming the two to be roped, one would have pulled off the other and both fallen uncontrollably. Wyn Harris was of a similar opinion. In a letter published by the Sunday *Times* in 1971, he wrote that if one of them had tumbled onto his back, the oxygen apparatus might have acted like the runners of a sledge, accelerating the plunge.

For years that seemed to be all we would ever know, especially as no Western mountaineers were allowed to visit the north side of Everest for almost three decades after the Chinese occupied Tibet. Meanwhile, however, in 1960, an announcement from Beijing claimed that a Chinese expedition had finally scaled the Northeast Ridge to the summit of Everest. Mountaineers in the West were skeptical; the Chinese had been climbing mountains for no more than five years, and the only reports released about the climb were couched in such ideological language that it was hard to pick a believable narrative from the clumsy translation and creative propaganda.

There were no summit photographs, as the three to reach the top—Qu Yinhua, Wang Fuzhou, and Gong Bu—did so in the dark. With their colleague Liu Lienman they had climbed the top section of Second Step, it was said, by combined tactics. Liu offered his shoulder to Qu, giving him just enough reach to hammer in two pitons to assist the ascent. Qu, chivalrously removed his studded boots before scrambling up on his friend. Once above the obstacle, he brought up his three companions on the rope; but the long delay without his boots left him severely frostbitten. And Liu was too exhausted to go on to the summit, so at the top of the Second Step he waited in his sleeping bag for their return.

Climbing the upper tier of the step, which is almost vertical and some 12 to 15 feet high had taken the four a full three hours. They removed their oxygen sets for the rock climbing, and indeed all the summiteers' oxygen ran out before the final pyramid was reached at 4:20 a.m. It was a bright day by the time they made it back down to Liu, and, before retreating down the Second Step, Qu, who had been entrusted with the expedition's little cine-camera, took two shots—one of the view of the mountains around, one back at the summit they had just left.

When the Chinese film reached London, the British 1933 veterans studied it carefully but could see nothing to convince them that the mountaineers really had climbed the mountain.

Family and friends of Mallory dedicated a stained glass window to his memory at a church in Mobberley. The central figure of St. George the dragon slayer may be designed to resemble George the mountain climber. A second panel depicting Sir Galahad recalls the nickname bestowed on Mallory by Geoffrey Young. To the world, however, it is windswept Everest that stands as Mallory's most lasting memorial.

Qu's panorama had been taken high, certainly, but no one could agree that it was from above the Second Step. It seemed so incredible to the Everest pioneers that a nation that had only just taken up mountaineering could have succeeded on a route that had defeated the more experienced British climbers. In 1975 the Chinese repeated the climb and made sure that this time the summit was filmed and a survey tripod left on top for others to find. They also placed a ladder to facilitate the climb of the upper tier of the Second Step. It was during this expedition that the late Wang Hung-bao stumbled across an "English dead," lying on the 27,000-foot terrace.

The news of his find was never publicly released—in fact it is still officially denied in Beijing—but rumors began circulating soon after the closed-door policy relaxd and foreign climbers were once more allowed into Tibet. Wang told his story to a Japanese climber, Ryoten Hasegawa, who passed it, via friends and contacts, to the world's press. Sadly, Wang was killed on the North Col, only a day after imparting his intriguing piece of information.

Wang had given a full description of the body to Hasegawa—but by means of sign language and characters scratched in the snow, as they did not share a language. Hasegawa understood Wang to mean that the body lay at 27,000 feet, had its knees drawn up, a hole in its cheek, and was dressed in tattered old-fashioned clothing that blew in the wind and disintegrated if you touched it.

These, then, were the clues in 1986 when we went to Everest to look for Mallory and Irvine: the ice ax, Odell's last sighting (which some disputed), and a suspect secondhand account of Wang's "English Dead." Only the ax could be called "hard" evidence, and its position was an estimate. No one is known to have rediscovered the ax Wyn Harris left in place of the original. Our expedition (organized by Andrew Harvard, Tom Holzel, and David Breashears) was unable to add to this evidence; the fall of 1986 was very windy and the snow deep, and our team did not get high enough to find anything. No other expedition went to the mountain specifically to conduct a search until the 1999 Mallory and Irvine Research Expedition, led by Eric Simonson.

Simonson later revealed a further clue. He remembered, on an earlier ascent of the mountain in 1991, seeing some very old oxygen bottles tucked under a rock about 300 feet below the First Step and above the level of the Yellow Band. They were at shoulder height in a spot described as "an obvious place for a climber to take a rest." In 1999, he dispatched members of his team to investigate. After some searching, they retrieved one rusty cylinder, which from its shape could only have come from the 1920s and from its location could only have been taken taken there by Mallory or

KING ARTHUR
SAINT GEORGE
SIR GALAHAD

Irvine. If it was stashed in the cranny by them (and not put up there later by climbers who found it lying nearby), it dispenses with the possibility that it fell from one of their carrying frames in an accident here. From the estimated position it appears to be below where the ice ax was found, but that site, too, was an estimate; there seems to have been no more than a few feet between them.

Simonson also wanted to know what could be seen of the ridge and its steps from where Odell stood on his rocky outcrop, when he caught his last inspiring glimpse of Mallory and Irvine in 1924. Andy Politz passed that way on the day they found Mallory's body. He gave his impressions to Liesl Clark, who was accompanying the expedition as part of the PBS/NOVA film team: "From where I stood I could see the three steps," he said to the camera. "Odell was supposed to have seen them climb to the top of one of the steps in five minutes....Well, I tell you, you're so magnetically drawn to the view and those three steps are definitely separated from that perspective." Politz did not feel it possible for any one of the rock steps to be mistaken for another and personally believed that the climbers must have been on the so-called Third Step when Odell saw them. "I think it's very obvious. What he described is clearly easy to define, even when the clouds part and you have just a few seconds of observation."

"The mighty summit...seemed to look down with cold indifference on me...and howl derision in wind-gusts at my petition to yield up its secret—this mystery of my friends," wrote Noel Odell on the disappearance of Mallory and Irvine.

THIS FINGERLESS INNER GLOVE AND LENGTH OF BROKEN ROPE WERE FOUND WITH GEORGE MALLORY'S BODY ON MAY 1, 1999.

CHAPTER EIGHT

I verily believe his death, as that of his well-loved and splendid companion, is a clarion call to our materialistic age, which so terribly needs the true unselfish spirit typified by George Mallory alike in his life and in its ending.

HOWARD SOMERVELL, 1924

READING THE CLUES

"All of a sudden, a patch of white, different from the snow and bright as marble, caught my eye. As I got closer I realized it was a person. Bleached white skin. A hobnailed boot. A braided climbing rope. No nylon." Conrad Anker was climbing with colleagues of the Mallory and Irvine Research Expedition on the morning of May 1, 1999, when he stumbled across his third body of the day. The two others had been wearing faded nylon high-altitude clothing and had relatively modern items of hardware; they were grotesquely crumpled, indicating that they had fallen a great distance to the sloping terrace. But this one was different. In his fuddled oxygen-starved state, Anker did not immediately register the significance of this man, lying facedown on the slope, his head pointing uphill, with both arms outstretched, as if grasping to arrest his slide.

"I sat down next to the body, studying the tattered edges of his wool sweater and cotton wind jacket....His right leg, broken above the ankle, was crossed over the left, perhaps to relieve the pain." Only then did the truth sink in: Anker had found one of the two climbers for whom his team was looking, but never really expecting to find. All he could think was "Wow!"

A skilled climber, Mallory is seen here on the Moine Ridge in the Alps in August 1909. In his memoirs, Sir Francis Younghusband—the British Armyman who snapped the first photo of Everest—said that members of London's Alpine Club, which sponsored the Everest expeditions, considered him "the finest climber they had."

When he and his fellow climbers fanned out across the terrace that morning, Anker had taken the lowest line, close to the terrace edge, somewhat outside their designated search area. Andy Politz had radioed to him, telling him he was looking too far down, but Anker was acting on a climber's intuition. He had been reading the subtleties of the terrain above, from where the other bodies had fallen through the Yellow Band, presumably all the way from the Northeast Ridge. This led him to a natural catchment basin for objects coming down from where it is believed Andrew Irvine's ice ax was found. A fluttering piece of brightly colored fabric drew his eye to the left, and just beyond this he spotted the bright patch of white, which turned out to be the bared back of the fallen man. Anker radioed his colleagues, and soon all four had joined him around the body.

At first, they took the victim to be Andrew Irvine; that is who they were expecting to find. He was firmly frozen into the slope, half-covered in gravel, with a severed climbing rope still tied around his waist and looped across one shoulder. He appeared well preserved—like "a Greek or Roman marble statue"—though the clothes on the upper, exposed side of his torso were in tatters. Inside his collar a name tag was stitched: "G. Mallory." Illogically, the search team's first thought was that Irvine was wearing Mallory's shirt, but another name tag and a monogrammed handkerchief convinced them that this really was Mallory himself. From his position and cruciform attitude, they felt fairly confident this was not the dessicated Englishman described by Wang Hong-bao in 1975 as being in a fetal position. It certainly looked as if this man had died where he lay, and remained undisturbed ever since; with his face hidden among stones, no one could have identified any "hole in his cheek," as Wang had observed of the corpse he'd seen. No, in all probability, it was Irvine Wang had stumbled across in 1975, higher up the slope. But if so, Anker and his colleagues were unable to locate that body.

A pair of snow goggles was found in one of Mallory's pockets; in others a packet of letters wrapped in a silk scarf, and miscellaneous notes and papers. There was a broken altimeter, scissors, a pocket knife, and a tin of beef lozenges, and in his trouser pocket a wristwatch with its hands missing. No trace could be found of his gloves, oxygen apparatus, or, more important, the Vestpocket Kodak camera he was believed to have borrowed from Howard Somervell.

Mallory appeared to have fallen from high on the tiered face above, more or less in a line from where the ice ax was found in 1933. By chipping away at some of the surrounding ice and rock, it was possible to ascertain that he

had sustained severe injuries, consistent with a sliding, tumbling fall. It is hard to imagine anyone surviving such a drop, and distressing to think of the great climber doing so; yet this man certainly looked as if he had, in a last moment of consciousness, flung wide his arms in one final lunge for life.

"The image that'll stick in my mind forever," Politz wrote on the Internet two days afterward, "is of this man fighting for his life right to the very end. He did not give up until he had stopped, and by then it would have been clear that there was no hope....I can just imagine him realizing that there was no chance of survival."

So at last there are a few more hard clues about what happened to Mallory and Irvine. Now, in addition to the ice ax, we know where Mallory's body lies, and have found a few other tangible relics, but still we have no easy answers. The goggles in the Mallory's pocket seem to suggest a descent in fading light or darkness, but there are other reasons why a high-altitude climber might not be wearing his goggles—a lens-clogging snow flurry, perhaps. Norton, as we know, removed his in normal daylight, simply because he could not see where to place his feet with them on. Much of one's field of vision was cut off by the metal rims and narrow, tinted lenses of those early goggles; and in fact, their design was changed for the 1933 British Everest Expedition. It is easy to say that Mallory, aware of Norton's subsequent snowblindness, would never have made the same "mistake," but faced with a similar problem he would know snowblindness to be a temporary consequence; the fall he was trying to prevent would be permanent.

The mystery of the circumstances under which the two men met with their fatal accident is no nearer to being solved; any more than is the perennially fascinating question of whether or not the two could have stood upon the summit. On the other hand, the great interest generated by this new discovery has ensured that we have almost as many elaborate theories as there are theorizers. Assuming Odell saw something on the ridge, but not knowing precisely where or what, the highest we could place Mallory and Irvine beyond any doubt before 1999 was the ice-ax site. That has not changed in the light of the 1999 findings.

The oxygen bottle found by Simonson's party is another hard clue, and confirms the two climbers were near the First Step. But whether they could have gone on to climb the much more challenging Second Step continues to be the difficult question, and can only be anwered in the context of what we know of the two days after Mallory and Irvine left the North Col.

June 7

There is nothing in the surviving record to tell us what time Mallory and Irvine arrived in Camp VI on June 7. But, from the experience of other parties, we would imagine them reaching the single tent in the rocky cleft within four to five hours of leaving Camp V—say, no later than noon. The note Mallory sends down to Odell tells us the weather is "perfect for the job." By that we take it that midday of the 7th, at least, is bright, not too cold, and windless. The pair will have another seven or so hours of daylight to prepare for their assault.

Irvine busies himself checking and fine-tuning the two oxygen sets they intend using. He will feel comfortable with this: It is what he has done throughout the expedition; you could almost say he has taken refuge in it. The fact that Odell, when he climbs up the next day, finds the tent strewn with an assortment of tools and spare parts does not of itself mean that one of the sets was malfunctioning. Nor that a last minute problem delayed the pair the next morning. The tent's disarray could be a manifestion of Irvine's almost compulsive tinkering, coupled with normal high-camp chaos. Very few climbers can cook, sleep, sort, and pack in a shared tight space without producing what Odell would call "an awful pickle."

What is Irvine thinking now that the porters have returned to the North Col? He and Mallory are completely on their own, cut off from the others until after their great effort. He might wonder if he's up to this climb. How can he know? Climbing to this camp, the exposed, intimidating ridge was in their sights for most of the morning. It would have been hard to judge what it would be like once they were up on it, but it looked forbidding and certainly more difficult than anything Irvine has climbed before. Even the sloping ground around the tent was awkward and insecure to walk on. Irvine lacked confidence in his fitness and ability; it would be natural for him to feel an element of apprehension now, some sense of "What have I got myself into?" But Mallory is counting on him, and he wants to live up to his friend's expectations. Besides, this should be a thrilling adventure. Perhaps it no longer matters that the time for saying "no" has passed; Irvine is caught up in the excitement and the vortex of Mallory, in whom he has utter faith. No one is better equipped for the task ahead than George, he thinks, nor more determined. No one deserves the summit more than George, after all the effort he's put in.

The irony is they are going for the summit with oxygen. Irvine has spent so much time on this trip trying to get enough serviceable sets together for an oxygen attempt, all the while hoping he will never be called upon to use it himself. "I would rather get to the foot of the final pyramid without oxygen," he told Odell, "than to the top with it!" Yet here he is, facing a summit day with just that unsettling prospect, when no one knows better than he how little trust can be placed in the cantankerous contraptions. That said, there is absolutely no reason to doubt his gameness to have his "whack."

His condition is something else again. We know his burned face is sheer agony, and peeling badly. We know in recent days he has had diarrhea, breathing difficulties, and a sore throat. But then, for anyone to feel fine at high altitude is a rare thing: Mallory has had a tearing cough, Somervell almost died a few days before from an obstruction in his throat. Up here, at Camp VI, Mallory is level with his old 1922 high point; he knows what to expect. But Irvine, in just two days, has climbed thousands of feet higher than he has been before, and the experience is all new: this breathlessness, the general malaise and sluggishness, the deadly dulling of all senses, even ambition.

Questions of whether or not Mallory and Irvine could have made it to Everest's summit hinge on their ability to surmount the Second Step, a steep wall just a few hundred feet below the top. A ladder erected by Chinese climbers makes it seem less than formidable (opposite), but a wider view shows how treacherous the terrain leading to the Second Step is.

And Mallory, what of him? He will be no less tense and excited. This is the culmination of his struggle with Everest. He came home from this mountain in 1921 professing delight that the highest snows were untrodden, but he doesn't think that now. He has promised Ruth and everyone he will climb this mountain. His quest to stand on the world's summit has claimed more than three years of his life, has given him status and purpose,and has made a folk hero of him. Yet he wants to be free to move on, to settle into his new job, to see his children grow. At the same time, he cannot turn his eyes or thoughts from Everest's summit.

We know now that Mallory's plan for that summit day was virtually impossible to achieve—in their optimism, early Everesters underestimated the challenges of summit day, particularly the lateral distance involved. It was not until 1990 that Ed Viesturs would climb to the summit and back from a camp near this position; all earlier successful parties placed their last camp higher and horizontally nearer the top. Still, from Mallory's point of view, he has never been better poised for a serious summit bid—even though he has wittingly handicapped himself. He has chosen, for this adventure, a comrade of strength, imbued with all the enthusiasm of youth, one moreover who looks up to him and trusts his judgement—a gratifying enough position in most circumstances. But, looking up at that long, rocky ridge now, Mallory cannot possibly consider he has selected the best climber for the task. There will come a point at which Irvine's follow-the-leader attitude is no longer a virtue, when Mallory needs a veteran climber at his side, rather than a disciple. He cannot call upon Irvine for a mountaineer's judgement; the two cannot share the decision making. Mallory has to assume responsibility for this innocent, willing conscript.

During the laborious ascent to Camp VI, Mallory will have been assessing his options; in the afternoon he may have wandered out to take a look at what they would face the next morning, but he is unlikely to have gone far. Norton has described what life in a high camp is like, when you flop exhausted into your sleeping bag the minute you arrive, and resist all calls to stir from it: "Then duty begins to call, one member of the party with groans and pantings and frequent rests crawls out of his bag, out of the tent and a few yards to a neighbouring patch of snow, where he fills two big aluminium pots with snow, what time his companion with more panting and groans sits up in bed, lights the meta burner and opens some tins and bags of food—say a stick of pemmican, some tea, sugar and condensed milk, a tin of sardines or bully beef and a box of biscuits. Presently both are again ensconced in their sleeping bags side-by-side with the Meta cooker doing its indifferent best to produce half a pot of warm water from each piled pot of powdery snow."

Mallory will be aware that on a ridge climb, you cannot always read the way ahead. Buttresses and pinnacles will obscure what lies beyond. Still, climbing at high altitude is always slow, providing enough pauses in which to continually review the route, and to look for weaknesses through or

BIG FOOTSTEPS

BY GEORGE MALLORY II

Several names will be linked forever with Mount Everest—Edmund Hillary, Tenzing Norgay, Reinhold Messner, Chris Bonington, and George Mallory. I did not choose my ancestry, and I have often wondered whether, given a choice, I would have elected to travel through life with the name I was given.

When I was a shy ten-year-old my father, John Mallory, donated a copy of David Robertson's biography of my grandfather to my primary school. The headmaster's speech to the assembled students, lauding George Mallory the heroic mountaineer, may have been entertaining for the other kids, but because I knew so little of what my grandfather had done, let alone the significance of his accomplishments, I was rather self-conscious about the attention directed my way. As a teenager in South Africa, I could still not grasp what Mallory had attempted though I did begin rock climbing, a sport I embraced with a passion. By 1987, I was a capable rock climber, and despite having made dozens of first ascents, the fact that I was the grandson of George Mallory, the legendary climber, remained a source of unease.

In 1994, I was invited to join an expedition to Everest's North Ridge. My only Himalayan experience, the ascent of a 19,680-foot peak, had aroused my curiosity and ignited my desire to attempt one of the "Himalayan giants," although the thought of blundering on the slopes of Everest terrified me.

Having committed myself to climbing Everest, I set about doing everything I could to ensure I would uphold the Mallory name. I devoted considerable energy to training for what I knew would be a very substantial physical challenge, and as I trained, I imagined my grandfather coaching me: "Listen George, if you want to climb Everest, you'll need to push yourself beyond utter exhaustion."

In May 1995, conditions on Everest's North Ridge were superb. Our expedition leader Paul Pfau had brought together a team of cautious mountaineers. We wanted to climb Everest, but were just as keen to return to our families, friends, jobs and lives. By mid-May we were poised at Camp VI, our highest camp at 27,200 feet, ready to have our go at the summit.

We set out at 1 a.m. There was not a breath of wind and the moon was full and bright as Jeff Hall, Chhiring Sherpa and I began our ascent. Conditions were perfect and we made rapid progress up the awkwardly sloping terrain. At 3:45 a.m. we reached the base of the Second Step. By then the moon, which had provided adequate light for climbing, was low in the western sky and we needed our headlamps. I attached my mechanical ascender to the fixed rope and, with some trepidation, started climbing up the steep corner that forms the lower section of the cliff.

A few minutes of climbing took me to a snow-covered ledge. Above was the fifteen-foot rock barrier that caps the Second Step. Thankfully the 1975 Chinese ladder was still in place.

Before launching myself up the ladder, I took a moment to look around and tried to imagine the challenge confronting Mallory in 1924: Had he and Andrew Irvine made it this far? Was their primitive oxygen apparatus working? As I examined the short cliff barring my way to the summit I became excited about what I saw; the rock wall offered several possible routes and I fleetingly wondered which one my grandfather would have chosen.

I resumed my ascent and by 4:00 a.m. the Second Step was beneath me. A sense of optimism replaced my anxiety about overcoming the technical difficulties and

I became intent on getting to the top as soon as possible. We negotiated another rocky outcrop without incident. Soon after that the sun rose and I watched the light spread across Nepal and Tibet.

At 5:30 a.m. we reached the spot from which we could climb no higher and I took in the majestic view from the summit which stretched 80 miles in every direction. The impact of the unexpected victory coupled with the stunning scenery was profoundly moving. At last, after years of uneasiness with my name and ancestry, a moment infused with the deepest meaning swept over me. I placed a photograph of my grandparents in the summit snow, knowing my grandfather would have been proud of me.

Many climbers would say that the summit is not worth a finger lost to frostbite. Others believe there are climbs for which it is worthwhile to risk injury, even death. Norton, Somervell, Mallory, and Irvine all took risks to prove it was possible to step onto the roof of the world. To all of them, these risks seemed worthwhile.

But for George Mallory's nearest and dearest and for Sandy Irvine's family, the premature deaths of these amazing men was then, and remains, a great tragedy.

GEORGE MALLORY II ATOP EVEREST, 1995

The families hopes for success and a safe return vanished into the mists. Left behind, in Mallory's case, were a widow with three young children. For Ruth, Clare, Beridge and John, June 1924 marked the beginning of life without George.

Before my ascent of Everest, I had been fascinated by the mystery surrounding the disappearance of Mallory and Irvine. Along with so many others, I was interested to know what happened to them. Had they reached the top? How did they die? When I returned to Melbourne it was with a deeper understanding and respect for the brave men and what they achieved. I soon came to understand there is really no need for an answer. In my view it is immaterial whether Mallory and Irvine succeeded or failed; what I admire is the spirit that drove them.

around the ridge's final rock barriers.

Always before, on the eve of a big climb, Mallory has written home, restating his devotion and debt to Ruth. So far as we know, on this last assault he writes to nobody, not even his "dearest girl." He carries letters in his pocket from family and a friend, which he probably intends to answer, but from everything that has been discovered since he was lost he appears to have sent no messages home since May 28.

Wanting to get a good start in the morning, the two will crawl into their sleeping bags early, but they are unlikely to manage more than brief snatches of sleep in the thin air. Finch, on his oxygen attempt in 1922, rigged up an apparatus to provide all three in his high camp with a small quantity of oxygen to allay distress throughout the night. He wrote afterward that there was no doubt it saved their lives. Norton and Somervell on the other hand professed to have slept reasonably well, even at this elevation. Mallory may well follow Finch's example here (as elsewhere), rather than take the risk of becoming prematurely exhausted like Norton and Somervell. This could account for the oxygen litter, the cylinder, and "spare parts" Odell later finds lying around the tent.

JUNE 8

The great day! Mallory, an early riser, will be up before first light. Norton and Somervell managed to get away by 6:40 a.m. when they left here on June 2 for their high climb; Norton expected Mallory to start even earlier, but it is doubtful if he and Irvine leave much before 6 o'clock.

However well prepared, in the flurry of leaving a tent, it is all too easy to miss items buried under clothes and sleeping bags. We know Mallory forgot his compass in the previous camp. When the debris of this camp is discovered by Longland and some porters in 1933, they retrieve a flashlight, which after nine years still shows a beam at the first press of a button. Perhaps it is a spare; but the suspicion remains that Mallory's chronic forgetfulness has robbed them of another survival tool.

They go out into the morning, which Odell tells us "broke clear and not unduly cold." Nonetheless, 1,500 feet higher than Odell, Mallory and Irvine will feel cold and sluggish to start. The sun will not hit the rocks until 8 o'clock. The cumbersome oxygen sets are "a bloody load for climbing." At this elevation, with or without bottled gas, you are reduced to the snail's pace Norton and Somervell have described. It is hard to manage much alacrity. Striking diagonally for the ridge, Mallory will follow the natural weaknesses in the Yellow Band. He will lead the pair over its downward-sloping slabs which, offering no good ledges or holds, climber Wyn Harris would describe in 1933 as being "evilly smooth and treacherous, where safety depends altogether on balance and the friction of the bootnails." There are places here requiring the use of one's hands to maintain balance. Wyn Harris, nevertheless, considered a rope "worse than useless" on this

The route and camps of the 1924 expedition—and the discoveries of the 1999 Mallory and Irvine Research Expedition—are mere filaments on the face of Everest. The location of Mallory's body clearly shows how far the fall was from his intended route.

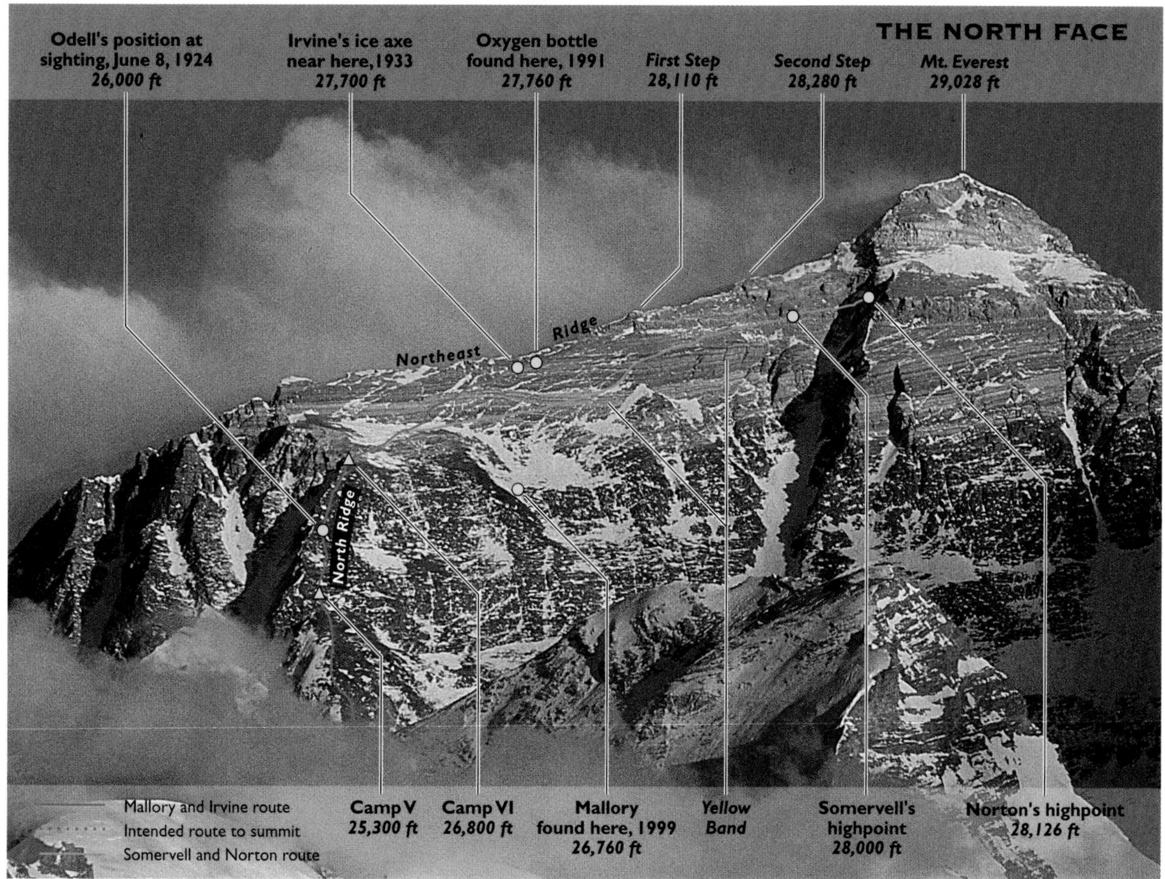

ground, even for loaded porters, since the slip of one man would pull his companions off. That said, it is reasonable to suppose Mallory, climbing with the inexperienced Irvine, is making use of the light rope they carry, to give his partner a greater sense of security.

As they near the crest of the Northeast Ridge, they start traversing west, keeping some 60 to 100 feet below its skyline to avoid unnecessary exposure to the 10,000-foot drop on the other side, the Kangshung Face. They pass the spot where the ice ax later will be found—which, from what we know, is close to where the 1999 team retrieved the vintage oxygen bottle, tucked under a small outcrop. Since the oxygen bottle's serial number matches with serial numbers Mallory had written on an envelope discovered on his body, we can assume that this is the spot where the pair paused to discard their first depleted bottles. Mallory had written to Odell they would probably go with two bottles each (the carrying frames could accommodate three); if he stuck with that, then they are already halfway through their day's oxygen supply, with only around four hours' climbing behind them.

As they approach the First Step, the day is still fine although patches of mist keep blowing across the North Face, obscuring the view down the mountain, and at times up the ridge. These mists are typical just prior to the onset of the monsoon, as rising warm currents meet colder air above and condense. Mallory will be keeping a watchful eye on any buildup of mist or cloud foreshadowing a storm that could obliterate their route of retreat and maroon them far from camp.

It is reasonable to conclude (based on later experience) that the pair reach this step at around 10 or 11 o'clock. What we will never know is how well their oxygen apparatus is functioning. It was apparently working well enough for them to use it to the point where the 1924 oxygen bottle was found. It's hard, however, to envision the sets performing flawlessly given the malfunctions and design flaws which plagued them. And it would be wrong to place too much emphasis on whether or not the apparatus was working efficiently, when any boost the gas could provide would be almost offset by the exceptional weight of these primitive sets.

Mallory has reached the spot where he must make his most important decision of the climb. He has a good, if foreshortened, view of the long ridgeline with many rocky steps and towers along its knife-edge. Is it a feasible route? With dismay, he perceives its unnerving exposure, and how much steeper it is than anything they have climbed so far. He looks at the formidable Second Step, of which all till now has been speculation. He always hoped there might be an easy way through it, but it's clear he cannot depend on that. Both Odell and Norton have reported fresh snow on the mountain that day: Norton calls it a "powdering"; Odell has a "considerable quantity covering some of the upper rocks near the summit ridge." Either will make the footing treacherous up there. Seen at close quarters, this ridge route that Mallory has always said he prefers loses its appeal.

In the message he sent to Captain Noel the previous day, Mallory told Noel to look out for them: "crossing the rockband under the pyramid or going up skyline." We cannot know what points of reference Mallory and Noel had agreed upon between them, but we can reasonably imagine they looked together at the summit section of the mountain, or studied one of Noel's telephotographs from the year before. The rock band under the pyramid is clearly recognizable (see page 189). Norton stood beneath it after crossing the Great Couloir a few days before, and reported that 200 feet higher, it would be possible to traverse to the right to gain the north face of the final pyramid and an easier gradient. In his opinion, it was only the time of day and his own shortness of breath that stopped him from continuing to the top. Mallory knows this; he will feel confident that he and Irvine, if they can get there earlier in the day, should be able to push higher. His note to Noel shows he is considering this as a possibility. In fact, by mentioning it first, you could read that this is his first option; that after what he saw yesterday, climbing up to Camp VI, he is already swinging toward the idea of going this way.

Below the ridge, a much easier-looking, sloping terrace now presents itself. This continues across the face, following the top of the

Retrieved from Mallory's pockets following the 1999 discovery of his body: snow goggles; an altimeter, missing its indicator hand; and a pocket knife, still operational and closed when found.

Yellow Band, to join the line of the traverse that Norton and Somervell followed toward the Great Couloir. To Mallory, standing here, it would offer the easiest, most obvious, most beguiling option by far; especially as it would gain them ground toward the summit relatively rapidly and safely.

By now, Mallory has a far better sense of what to expect from Irvine, his confidence and climbing power, and indeed how much liability his inexperience represents—all factors to affect his decision. Irvine, too, can see what the ridge entails. If he has qualms about tackling it, he can say so. [Modern climbers who have followed this route describe it as tricky, steep, and deceptive, requiring a lot of care, saying also that it is difficult to come down.]

The dilemma facing Mallory now would be confronted by Wyn Harris and Wager nine years later. They reached this spot, intending to follow "Mallory's Ridge" to the Second Step. Tough and experienced climbers both, they took one look up at the two large towers that comprise the First Step, serrated ridge, and the "impregnable" Second Step, about 200 yards away, and abandoned their plan. "It would be far easier," they said, "to traverse along the top of the yellow band...horizontally westwards, over snow-covered slabs, keeping roughly to the line where the Yellow Band adjoins the bottom of the dark-grey limestone precipice forming the continuation of the First Step." It was a sensible mountaineering decision, and it is hard to imagine Mallory concluding differently, especially with clouds beginning to well up from below. But, whichever of these divergent routes he ultimately takes, Mallory wants to be confident that every step gained can eventally be reversed. He knows that climbing down is invariably more difficult and dangerous than climbing up. And once the choice is made, they will be committed; they cannot switch from one to the other, once started.

If we believe Mallory and Irvine take the terrace option (and why, if they are wanting to climb a virgin mountain, go for anything other than the line of least resistence?), it requires us to relinquish once and for all the idea that Odell saw them on the Second Step. On this route, we would expect them to reach Norton's high point by about 1:00 p.m., but (with the benefit of hindsight and despite Mallory's expectations) probably no further. In 1933, Wyn Harris, Wager, and Frank Smythe were all turned back from the slabs on the western wall of the Great Couloir at approximately the same height as Norton, even though (like him) they thought it should be possible to go further with the rocks dry and free of snow. Those would not be, however, the conditions Mallory and Irvine would find.

If, on the other hand, we prefer to believe Mallory remains wedded to his ridge, despite all, how does his day progress from here? The ridge is steep-sided, making for awkward traversing. Even an easy-angled traverse, though not technically difficult, presents more challenge than steeper terrain where footholds are good. The danger of a slip is ever present, and climbers gain no security (psychologically or in real terms) from their rope—there being anywhere from 15 to 100 horizontal feet of line separating them and no way of securely anchoring it. Tying himself to Irvine here, where a fall of one means the fall of both, Mallory is reducing his safety factor to the ability of his friend. He is pinning his faith in Irvine's competence to move over difficult ground—knowing that however stout and strong this young oarsman is, he lacks the grace and confidence of the experienced climber. Irvine is bound to be tentative climbing on the insecure terrain, and slower to progress. We know from many accounts how swiftly and fluidly Mallory can move; how impatient he can be of fellow climbers who cannot match his frantic pace. Will he urge Irvine on as time slips away, or will he shrink his ambition to match the circumstances? It's probably close to 1:00 p.m. He must see his summit chances diminishing. If they are on their last oxygen bottle, it is hard to imagine there being much gas left by this time; and if they are still weighed down with the oxygen apparatus, these slithery, snow-covered slabs become particularly hazardous. Besides, the rolling banks of mist of Odell's have thickened now, bringing snow flurries. And the wind is rising. Even if the climbers are above the mists, as Odell supposed, Mallory will be alarmed to see dense cloud billowing up the face.

If we want to postulate that the pair made it as far as the foot of Second Step, it is hard to give credence to any theory that has them attempting to climb it. This steep and daunting obstacle has tremendous exposure. It blocks the ridge entirely; Mallory will find there is no way of going around it; the end drops sheer away down the face. Beforehand, he may have pictured himself forcing a brilliant line through its defenses, just as he has on so many technically more difficult crags, but confronting it now, the reality will dash that dream. Even if he could make it himself, how is he to get Irvine up, and later down, such a pitch, when the latter has spent no more than a handful of days rock climbing in his life? There is a threshhold that, if a climber passes it, he knows he has gone beyond safe retreat; the Second Step represents such a threshhold for Mallory, and it is hard to imagine he would elect to go for broke with Irvine at his side. He will not be oblivious to his partner's limitations; he has been watching him carefully throughout the expedition, sharing his observations with Ruth as recently as May 16. "Against him," he said, "is his youth—hard things seem to hit him a bit harder—and his lack of mountain training and practice which must tell to some extent when it comes to climbing rocks or even to saving energy on the easiest ground." Geoffrey Young once warned Mallory, "Your weakness, if any, is that you...do not hold back from allowing yourself to sweep weaker brethren, carried away by their belief in you, to take risks or exertions that they were not fit for." But that was many years ago. Up here, the debilitatingly thin atmosphere is the moderator.

No climber becomes more exceptional as the air becomes thinner; even great climbers are reduced to what Reinhold Messner describes as, "a single gasping lung." Standing under the formidable wall of the Second Step, Mallory again has to consider Irvine's ability. He knows enthusiasm will get you out of your tent, but it cannot substitute for skills *(continued on page 232)*

THE DAY THEY FOUND MALLORY

BY LIESL CLARK

It was a triumphant moment. As the light faded from the mountains behind them, painting the upper slopes of Mount Everest in shades of crimson, our team of climbers strode across the flat, sandy moraine to Base Camp like astronauts returning from the Moon. Each looked a little thinner and sunburned from 10 days above 21,000 feet. Just 72 hours earlier, at 26,770 feet, Conrad Anker had found the body of George Leigh Mallory.

As they came near, I saw a look in their eyes that I will never forget. Five climbers had stepped back into history and returned changed. They were the first to discover the truth: that George Mallory fell to his death on his summit day, while climbing roped to Andrew Irvine. The team found Mallory lying face down, arms outstretched, his hands clenched to the frozen surface of the mountain. He had apparently tried to arrest his fall with his hands and came to rest on a sloping, rock-strewn ledge on the North Face of Everest. The thin rope that had joined him to Irvine was broken.

At the time of the discovery, we had been on Everest for more than a month. I was there to direct a documentary for the PBS science series, NOVA. The film would follow an expedition searching for the bodies of Mallory and Irvine, led by veteran Everest climber, Eric Simonson. The team had chosen the dry, spring pre-monsoon season for their ascent. This year conditions on the mountain were especially ideal for a search: the lack of snowfall and a relentless scouring by jet-stream winds had left Everest's slopes absolutely bare.

MALLORY'S HOBNAILED BOOT

On April 30th, Simonson's handpicked team reached Camp V. Teammates Dave Hahn, Andy Politz, Tap Richards, Conrad Anker, and Jake Norton were poised for the final, high-altitude push to their designated search area. In 1975, Chinese climber, Wang Hong-bao, had reported finding a body at about 27,000 feet. No one had ever expressly climbed to this location to search for the mysterious "English dead" Wang discovered. Now our team had targeted this site, and an adjacent area in the fall line below the site high on Everest's North East Ridge where Irvine's ice axe had been found in 1933.

At 5 a.m. on May 1st, we received the first radio call to Base Camp. "We're good to go," reported climber Dave Hahn, as he readied himself at Camp V. "We're putting on our crampons." "Did you sleep well?," we radioed back. "Negative," Hahn replied crisply. "We didn't come here to sleep. We came to climb and search."

THE 1999 MALLORY AND IRVINE RESEARCH EXPEDITION ON THE PANG LA

On the previous night I had been apprehensive about the upcoming search. Light puffs of wind rustled the walls of my tent, like whispers from the ghosts of Everest. After 75 years, would we find any evidence of Mallory or Irvine high on Everest? At dawn the gusts turned more insistent. As the sun rose blasts of cold penetrated my thick down jacket, and I wondered how much colder it would be at 27,000 feet, our climbers' destination.

At 9:20 a.m. we aimed our powerful telescope and spotted the climbers moving slowly across tilted slabs of loose rock toward the snow terrace where the Chinese expedition had placed their Camp VI in 1975. The site was to be our team's starting point. There weren't many clues to guide the climbers, but Hahn, Anker, and the others were familiar with the general search area, and each navigated by his own intuition.

Ten thousand feet below, we heard Anker radio his search mates: "Can you see what I'm pointing at on the ledge?" Moments passed; we could only guess at what he saw. Then Tap Richards came on the radio: "I've found two bodies at the base of the fall line. I see red, white and blue nylon on one and a jumar [mechanical ascender] on the other. So I think they're at least 20 years old."

We watched as the climbers split the search area in three areas, with Anker on the bottom of the snow terrace; Politz at the base of the Yellow Band; and Hahn, Richards, and Norton in between. In less than an hour, Anker radioed his companions again. We were puzzled by the odd transmission fragments we periodically intercepted: "Why don't you come down for Snickers and tea?" Then, more insistent: "Mandatory group meeting."

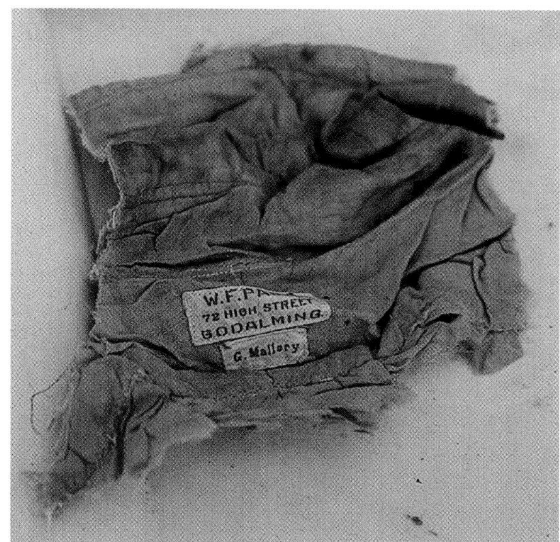

MALLORY'S WEATHERED INNER GARMENT

As we peered through the telescope, it became evident that the cryptic radio transmissions were signals. We watched as the five climbers assembled on the bottom edge of the snow terrace where Conrad waited. What was "Snickers and tea" a code for? And why were they huddled on the terrace? Aware that other expeditions could listen in on our frequency, we had all previously agreed to keep the radio transmissions to a minimum if a body were found. This "mandatory meeting" which sent the team down to a ledge, out of the boundaries of the original search area, could only mean Anker had found something important." I was going up the hill and I was zigzagging in sort of a pattern," Anker later explained, "I glanced over to my right and noticed a patch of white that wasn't rock and it wasn't snow. As I started traversing closer I saw what appeared to be the lower part of a leg, and it was a heel. I climbed nearer and suddenly saw hobnailed boots and old clothing"

It was a leather boot that caught his eye, Anker later said. This antique boot he recounted, "was my first indication that I had come upon either Mallory or Irvine." The sight of old-fashioned layers of natural fiber clothing, torn by the impact of Mallory's fall, also suggested that the body was from an earlier era.

"We didn't know it was George at first," Dave Hahn told us, "because all the assumptions were that it was Sandy's body," referring to the 1975 find. "Jake found this clothing label on the neck," Hahn continued. He pulls this 'G. Mallory' tag out...bringing me a little closer to 20th-century history than I ever thought I'd be. And it took me a few seconds to understand that. It came as quite a shock."

The enthralled team spent an hour examining Mallory and gathering artifacts. "He had fractures of his leg bones," Hahn recounted. "He had a broken arm on the right side, and trauma to his shoulder. You could see this was a fall. You could see where the rope had bit into him, but it wasn't excessive trauma. He was at nearly 27,000 feet; he was wearing nothing by our standards. He was going to die of exposure with such trauma."

It was hard for the search team, and for me, to grasp that the team had found George Mallory and not Andrew Irvine. It was Irvine's ice ax that had been found at 27,700 feet, and climbers had assumed that it had been the inexperienced Irvine who'd fallen, not the legendary mountaineer George Mallory. But the name

ANDY POLITZ EXAMINES THE REMNANTS OF MALLORY'S CLOTHING AT BASE CAMP

tags in Mallory's clothing and the astonishing discovery of letters addressed to George Leigh Mallory, Esq., found in his pockets left no doubt. "My Dearest George," began the hand-written letters from his sister, Mary, and his younger brother Trafford.

But what had happened to Irvine? Would the artifacts shed light on Mallory and Irvine's summit attempt? There was no camera found with Mallory. Only goggles, an altimeter, a watch, a knife and other items commonly carried by Himalayan climbers of the day. Did the hands of Mallory's altimeter, now broken, ever point to 29,028 feet?

As we drove from Base Camp, bumping over the stones of the moraine, our jeeps plunging one last time through the silt-laden glacial streams, we knew little more about whether Mallory or Irvine had summitted.

My own thoughts flashed back to 1924, when Noel Odell, Captain John Noel, and the other members of Mallory's fateful expedition returned home over this same terrain, contemplating the loss of their two companions. Like us, they must have replayed over and over the possible final steps of Mallory and Irvine. The mystery about their summit attempt remains unsolved, but the strength of Mallory's desire to be the first is clear: "How you will hope that I was one of the conquerors!" Mallory wrote to his wife Ruth on April 19, 1924. "And I don't think you will be disappointed."

and experience you don't have. Despite his fierce determination to succed, "[We'll] stamp to the top with our teeth in the wind," Mallory surely recognized the futility and recklessness in climbing higher. He was driven, maybe even obsessed, but he was not fanatical. Somervell neatly expressed the sentiment of the early Everest climbers when he remarked, "We were willing of course to risk our lives, but we thought it wrong to throw them away."

It is hard to know what time the pair set for themselves to turn around to ensure reaching their high camp before dark, but if they want to get down to Camp IV—as Mallory mentioned in his note to Odell—they must soon start thinking about it. In darkness it would have been almost impossible to find their tiny tent, perched for protection behind a rock outcrop. The possibility of an open bivouac was never a consideration in their summit plans. They know, equipped as they were, that spending a night out in the open above 27,000 feet would mean almost certain death. With the summit seemingly within grasp, Mallory realizes he must turn back; his long quest is over.

The blizzard that struck Odell as he reached Camp VI blew in at around 2 o'clock that afternoon and raged for a couple of hours. It was not so vicious as to prevent Odell from scrambling about on the North Face, yodelling and whistling to give direction to Mallory and Irvine, who he thought might be retreating. But the stiff wind and driving sleet forced him at last to huddle behind a rock to escape its fury. "One could not see more than a few yards ahead so thick was the atmosphere," he later wrote. We can be certain that if this storm hit Odell on the mountainface, it will have blasted Mallory and Irvine on the ridge a thousand feet higher, where it would be windier and colder. Odell may have hoped they were above it, but from all the fresh snow he saw up there afterward, that clearly was not so.

Afternoon storms are a feature on Everest; this would not be unlike the one encountered by Jack Longland in 1933, when he was trying to shepherd a band of porters between that expedition's Camps VI and V. "Without any warning that I remember," Longland has written, "a great storm blew up out of the west. There weren't any more distant horizons—the most I could see was a snow-swept circle of twenty or thirty yards....The snow began to cover the holds on the rocks, and give a slippery coating to the patches of scree, and the wind came in rather terrifying gusts, forcing us to cling or cower against the rocks to avoid being blown bodily away."

Up on the ridge, Mallory and Irvine would have been exposed to the full force of the squall with no protection from driving sleet and wind. If Mallory has not already made the decision to turn back, this sudden blizzard will surely clinch matters. He will want to get himself and Irvine off this spot. He will not know how long the storm might last; and always one to prefer action over waiting, Mallory, like Longland, will surely press on down, through the teeth of it. Route-finding in poor visibility will be extremely difficult, but not impossible; they must keep well down from the crest as they did coming up, but it only takes an

No hands remain on Mallory's watch, but rust marks intriguingly seem to place its final time at 5:10. The crystal was broken, probably in his fatal fall. The matches were almost certainly for the high camp stove. The tin of meat lozenges promised "Portable Nourishment at all Times."

inch of snow to cover what few tracks they left and to obscure the best places to put their feet. This sloping traverse will be lethal now; and wet snow and ice will soon clot their faces and find their way into every chink and layer of their clothing. Longland again gives us insight: "My snow-goggles soon became quite useless, choked with snow," he recounted. "I took them off, only to find that eyelids and eyelashes coated up as well, forming an opaque film which had to be rubbed away every few minutes before I could peer out again and get a glimpse of the next few yards."

Low visibility brings the climber a double handicap: Not only is it hard to see where he is going, communication becomes difficult with his companion. This is a blueprint for disaster, yet it cannot account for the Mallory and Irvine tragedy. From the position of Mallory's body (unless the pair had fallen that morning on their way up the mountain, which seems unlikely), they must have retreated a considerable distance from their high-point before they fell—whether that point was on the ridge, in the Great Couloir, or even higher. They will have picked their way laboriously down and across the mountain in nightmare conditions. The descent is now a struggle for survival—they must keep moving, or freeze.

As they get lower and back on to the discontinuous ridges of the Yellow Band, finding the route becomes harder. It may be necessary to backtrack, try different lines, over and again. The fresh snow will make it hard to tell where any ledge starts and ends. This yellow limestone is streaked through with veins of a whitish, quartzy rock that is very slippery. Smythe spoke of it in 1933: "To a tired man this rock forms a trap, for the foot slips from it more easily than it does from the yellow rock."

We can picture the ground but never know what prompted the fatal slip, or which of them fell first. The causes of accidents in mountaineering, especially during the descent, are often as mundane as tripping over the rope, making a simple misstep—a momentary lapse of concentration by a weary climber returning from a high adventure, hoping to reach camp safely, and looking forward, at the end of an expedition, to going home to family and friends.

On those low-angled slabs, a slide will start slowly, innocently almost, yet the dreadful realization will follow fast, as the climber picks up speed, that he is not going to stop. The first his companion will know of the fall is a gasp or shout, a scraping of hobnails or ax; and he too will instantly know the sick shock of inevitability. He has to drop his ax, grab the rope, brace for the inevitable jolt, but it will be hopeless. When he is tugged from his feet, he and his partner both know it's the end. They slide and bump and bounce down the Yellow Band, all their hopes for a safe retreat lost in one swirling, disorienting tumble. And the disbelief. No one will know what they achieved this day. No more messages of love can be sent. All those things they wanted to say, to do, to be...will never now be said or done. One moment of fatigue has translated into terror.

As each climber comes to a sliding halt, we have to hope oblivion does not follow far behind.

George Mallory's body does not appear to lie plumb below the accepted ice-ax site, but some distance toward the east. Of course, the position we have for the ax is only an estimate. A slight adjustment to this, and a careful study of the precise configuration of that part of the North Face, its slopes and deflecting surfaces, could well account for the anomaly. What is difficult to square, however, is the lack of severe damage to the body. Enough trauma to kill a man, certainly, but not to suggest that he has fallen from the ridge or close under it where the ice ax was found over 900 feet above. The attitude of the body suggests that in the last moments of consciousness George Mallory was able to roll over and straighten his pose before dying. It leads to speculation that Mallory was further down the Yellow Band, well below the ice ax, when he and Irvine fell. Dave Hahn, one of the search team, is sure of it. "This man had fallen in the rocks," he said, "and then he must have slid some distance down snow slopes, but he'd lived through it all. He'd arrested his fall with outstretched arms and grasping hands and he'd composed himself to die, crossing his broken leg over the other to get some last relief."

Odell, we know, went out and looked again for Mallory and Irvine once the storm had blown itself out. He saw nothing. And later, on his way back to the North Col, he stopped frequently as his vantage point improved to scan the face for any trace of the pair. Neither then, nor later that evening when he and Hazard kept intermittant lookout from the North Col in the moonlight, were any distress signals to be seen. It is one of life's ironies that he saw climbers earlier in the day, when many experts maintain he shouldn't have been able to pick out anything from his viewpoint; then, when you would expect him to have spotted movement on the face, toward evening, when the weather was clear and bright, he saw nothing.

No matter how you assemble these clues you hit anomalies and more questions—nothing fits neatly to give irrefutable answers. Even the two firm pieces of evidence—the ax and the body—cannot be linked by a single fall. If Odell did not see the climbers returning to Camp VI, was that because they were much higher after all, or because they were already dead? It seems unlikely they would have fallen in the morning, though not impossible of course: The apparatus is cumbersome, the ground underfoot sloping and insecure. Yet, if they did not fall from the position of the ice ax, why is the ax there? And if Mallory and Irvine perished on June 9 while descending from a cripplingly cold bivouac forced by a late-afternoon descent, as some suggest, then it's likely Mallory's fingers and toes would be frostbitten. They aren't.

Suppose, after all, Odell really did see the men at the top of Second Step, or above—a very slim option admittedly, given anticipated timings—how do we conclude they climbed it? We know that in 1960 it took inexperienced but highly motivated and fit Chinese climbers three hours to get up the Second Step. And we no longer doubt that they did so. It seems the evidence was there all along in the Chinese film, and we missed it. Qu Yinhua, after rejoining Liu Lienman at the top of the Second Step, turned around and with the Party cine-camera took one short, medium-angle shot looking back at the summit. It's a wobbly, over-exposed shot, but for a fraction of a second there appears on the left-hand edge of the frame the rocks of the diminutive Third Step. He could not have taken such a picture from anywhere below the Second Step. Western mountaineering owes China an apology for doubting their ascent of, what is now known as the Mallory Route on Everest. But did they ascend it first?

It is tempting to suppose that if the Chinese could climb the Second Step, albeit with combined tactics and the use of two or three pitons, Mallory could also have done so. From here the summit would look tantalisingly close. That is a deception, but how could he know that? If he and Irvine had come so far, would they turn back now? Despite his respect for Mallory, Conrad Anker, who avoided the fixed rope and climbed the Second Step using only one rung of the Chinese ladder, is convinced that a climber of the 1920s, however skilled, could not have surmounted that great obstacle.

Most people like to think they succeeded; many believe it, but it takes an act of faith. The trouble with making optimistic timings based on oxygen-flow rates and postulated climbing speeds, which would have enabled Mallory and Irvine to have climbed the Second Step, and possibly also the summit, unfortunately ignores basic truths. They would not have been following a well-documented line, but route-finding, which is inevitably slower. The upper slopes we know were plastered with fresh snow, and they could surely not have climbed upward through Odell's squall. And how can we know, in that unforgiving atmosphere, how strong or debilitated they were feeling that day. Irvine has climbed from 23,000 feet—5,000 feet higher than he has ever been—in two and a half days. What effect did this have on his physical performance and mental acuity. But most obvious of all: Mallory was a mountaineer, and when it mattered most, he could be expected to make crucial decisions on their mountaineering merit, rather than personal ambition. And in any case, ambition is one of the first casualties of high altitude.

We can never know exactly what happened on June 8, 1924. Even if someday the discovery of a small camera with precious images might show us that Mallory and Irvine miraculously stood upon the summit of the world, 29 years before Hillary and Tenzing, it can never tell us what caused the fatal plunge. It might, just possibly, prove which route they took above the First Step. But perhaps, all this emphasis on the summit, is to miss the point entirely. The deaths of these two heroes—for surely that is what they were—remind us of a time when there

George Mallory is commemorated by his son John and grandson George Mallory II, who placed a memorial stone close to Base Camp in 1995. An earlier anonymously placed plaque also marks the spot. Behind them, Everest's summit is swathed in clouds as it guards clues to the decades-old mystery of Mallory and Irvine.

were still triumphant moments of exploration on this planet, when it was possible to walk off the map—when the slopes of the world's highest peak were untrodden and the shape of the great mountain could only be imagined. A time before orbiting satellites and the wonders of GPS revealed our world in such technical clarity. There were great adventures and discoveries for those who would seize the opportunity, take the risks. Somervell saw their deaths as "a clarion call to a materialistic age"—75 years later, in a world more materialistic than Somervell or Mallory could ever have dreamed, we can still admire the driving spirit of these men of the pioneer expeditions. They forsook comfort and security of family and home in their quest for Earth's supreme height. Primitive as their gear seems to us today, and limited their knowledge of the mechanics of high-altitude mountaineering, they were equipped with an ardour for discovery that took them to the limits of human achievement. Although Mallory and Irvine perished for their dream, they showed the way, and helped us understand both the tug of Everest, and the indomitable nature of the human spirit. Their achievement is so much greater than our need to know whether or not they climbed to the top.

INDEX

ILLUSTRATIONS CREDITS

Cover (background): John Noel Photographic Collection
Cover (inset): Salkeld Collection
Back Cover: John Noel Photographic Collection
Front Matter: 1, Mallory/Irvine Expedition/Jim Fagiolo/Liaison Agency; 2-3, John Noel Photographic Collection; 4-10 (both), The Alpine Club; 11-12, John Noel Photographic Collection. Introduction: 14, Clare Millikan, Salkeld Collection. Prologue: All by David Breashears. Chapter One: 26-28 (both), National Portrait Gallery, London; 30, The Alpine Club, photo by Geoffrey Young; 31, Salkeld Collection; 33, Clare Millikan; 34-35, Royal Geographical Society (RGS), photo by John Claude White; 38-39, The Illustrated London News Picture Library; 41, The British Library; 46-47, John Noel Photographic Collection; 49, George Ingle Finch Collection; 50 (left), Salkeld Collection; 50 (right), Irvine Archive. Chapter Two: 52, Norton Everest Archive; 54-55, The Alpine Club; 56-57, RGS, photo by John Noel; 59 (both), RGS, photos by George Mallory; 60-61, The Alpine Club; 62, RGS, photo by A.F.R. Wollaston; 65, George Ingle Finch Collection; 66-67, RGS, photo by George Mallory; 69, RGS; 70-71, RGS, photo by George Mallory; 73 (upper), Salkeld Collection, photo by George Mallory; 73 (lower), RGS, photo by George Mallory; 74-75, RGS, photo by Col. C.K. Howard-Bury; 77, RGS, photo by Guy Bullock; 78-79, RGS, photo by George Mallory. Chapter Three: 80, RGS, photo by T. Howard Somervell; 83 (upper), RGS, photo by George Mallory; 83 (lower), RGS, photo by John Noel; 84-85, The Alpine Club; 87-89 (both), John Noel Photographic Collection; 91 (upper), The Alpine Club, photo by George Ingle Finch; 91 (lower), T. Howard Somervell; 92-93, The Alpine Club; 94-95, John Noel Photographic Collection; 96, T. Howard Somervell; 98-99, John Noel Photographic Collection, photo by Bentley Beetham; 100-101, The Alpine Club; 103, George Ingle Finch Collection; 104, George Ingle Finch Collection; 104-105, Mallory/Irvine Expedition/Jim Fagiolo/ Liaison Agency; 105, George Ingle Finch Collection; 106, RGS, photo by John Noel; 107 (upper), George Ingle Finch Collection; 107 (lower), The Alpine Club, photo by George Ingle Finch; 108-109, George Ingle Finch Collection; 111, Ken Wilson Collection, photo by A.W. Wakefield; 112, RGS, photo by T. Howard Somervell; 113-115 (both), George Ingle Finch Collection. Chapter Four: 116, Salkeld Collection; 119 (upper), Irvine Archive; 119 (lower), The Times Picture Library; 120, RGS, photo by N.E. Odell; 123-127 (all), RGS, photo by Bentley Beetham; 128-129, Salkeld Collection, photo by N.E. Odell; 130, Norton Everest Archive; 132-133, John Noel Photographic Collection; 135, The Times Picture Library; 136-138 (all), John Noel Photographic Collection; 139, George Ingle Finch Collection; 141, RGS, photo by Bentley Beetham; 142, Salkeld Collection, photo by N.E. Odell; 143, RGS, photo by John Hazard. Chapter Five: 144, T. Howard Somervell; 147, John Noel Photographic Collection; 148-149, RGS, photo by Bentley Beetham; 150, The Times Picture Library; 152-153, John Noel Photographic Collection; 154, George Ingle Finch Collection; 155, RGS, photo by T. Howard Somervell; 158, T. Howard Somervell; 161, RGS, photo by John Noel; 163-167 (all), T. Howard Somervell. Chapter Six: 168, RGS; 171-173 (both), RGS, photo by Bentley Beetham; 174-175, The Alpine Club; 178-179, The Times Picture Library, photo by John Noel; 181, RGS, photo by T. Howard Somervell; 182-183, The Alpine Club; 184-185, RGS, photo by N.E. Odell; 185, John Noel Photographic Collection; 186, Keith Barclay; 188-189, The Times Picture Library; 189-191 (all), John Noel Photographic Collection. Chapter Seven: 192, NGS News Collection; 195, RGS; 196-197, Norton Everest Archive; 198, The Times Picture Library; 201, John Noel Photographic Collection; 202, The Sandy Irvine Trust, photo by Julie Steele; 205, Mark Thiessen, National Geographic Photographer; 206, The Alpine Club; 209, Ken Wilson; 210-211, RGS, photo by Bentley Beetham. Chapter Eight: 212, Mallory/Irvine Expedition/Jim Fagiolo/Liaison Agency; 215, The Alpine Club; 218 (upper), Mstislave Gorbenko; 218 (lower), Photo by Daqiong, courtesy The Mountaineering Association of Tibet, China; 221, Courtesy George Mallory II; 223, Galen Rowell/Mountain Light; 225, Mallory/Irvine Expedition/Jim Fagiolo/Liaison Agency; 228, Thom Pollard; 229, Liesl Clark; 230, Thom Pollard; 231, Liesl Clark; 233, Mallory/Irvine Expedition/Jim Fagiolo/Liaison Agency; 237, David Breashears.

Published by the National Geographic Society
145 17th Street N.W., Washington, D. C. 20036

First Printing, October 1999

Library of Congress Cataloging-in-Publication Data

Breashears, David.
Last climb : the legendary Everest expeditions of George Mallory / David Breashears and Audrey Salkeld ; introduction by John Mallory.
p. cm.
Includes index.
ISBN 0-7922-7538-1
1. Leigh-Mallory, George Herbert, 1886-1924. 2. Mountaineers--Great Britain Biography. 3. Mountaineering--Everest, Mount (China and Nepal) I. Salkeld, Audrey. II. Title. III. Title: Legendary Everest expeditions of George Mallory.
GV199.92.L44B74 1999
796.52'2'092--dc21
[B]
99-41046
CIP

Printed in U.S.A.

ACKNOWLEDGEMENTS

Over our long research into the early climbing history of Mount Everest, very many friends have helped with information and advice. But no telling of this story could begin without the contemporary expedition books and the journals of the Alpine Club and the Royal Geographical Society, who jointly sponsored this early exploration. Nor could any study of George Mallory be written without leaning heavily on earlier biographical works by David Pye and David Robertson.

But for so much of the personal documentation, photographs and permission to quote from diaries and letters, we are indebted to the families of the Everest pioneers. Our special thanks go to the Mallory family: John Mallory, Clare Millikan, George Mallory II, Frank and Virginia Arnott, and the late Barbara Newton-Dunn; and to Andrew Irvine's relatives: Peter and Bill Summers, Julie Steele and the late Alec Irvine. Also: Sally Amos and Sylvia Branford (daughters of Dr. Longstaff), Sandra Noel, Bill and Dick Norton, Ian Morshead, Peter Odell, Anne Russell (daughter of G.I. Finch), David Somervell, Keith Barclay (nephew of J. de Vars Hazard), Elizabeth Osborne (grand-daughter A.W. Wakefield), and the Misses Maureen and Jill Hingston.

We owe a big debt to Tom Holzel, without whose preoccupying urge to discover the fate of Mallory and Irvine, we would not have gone to Everest in 1986 and might not be writing this book now; and to our dear friends and fellow Everesters Andrew Harvard and Graham Hoyland who have been a constant source of encouragement and advice. Shrewsbury School's exhibition in 1999 to celebrate the life of former student Andrew Irvine, was not only tasteful and interesting in itself but helped to recover important Irvine memorabilia; Stephen Holroyd and his team are to be thanked and congratulated for this memorable event. Conrad Anker shared with us his experiences on the 1999 Research Expedition. The researcher Jochen Hemmleb has helped to cast fresh light on old conundrums. We would also like to thank the 1960 Chinese summitteers, Qu Yinhua, Wang Fuzhou and Gongbu, who have so willingly and helpfully answered our questions.

Irvine's Everest diary is at Merton College, Oxford; Finch's at the National Library of Scotland; and there is a large collection of Mallory letters at Magdalene College Cambridge. We saw Shebbeare's diary at the Alpine Club (where we are grateful to Livia Gollancz and Bob Lawford for all their assistance), and Bentley Beetham's photographs at Barnard Castle School, courtesy of Michael Lowes of the Old Barnardians. We are grateful, too, for the help of Joanna Scaddon in the Picture Library of the Royal Geographical Society and Fiona Mieklejon of *The Times* Picture Library.

For their forbearance while our attentions were perennially elsewhere we are grateful to Liesl Clark and Peter Salkeld. Finally, we wish to commend the encouragement and support of Kevin Mulroy, our sage and patient editor; our designer Lisa Lytton, and the good folk at National Geographic who pulled out all stops for us. This has been a cooperative effort. Thank you, all.

LAST CLIMB
The Legendary Everest Expeditions of George Mallory
DAVID BREASHEARS AND AUDREY SALKELD

Published by the National Geographic Society
JOHN M. FAHEY, JR. *President and Chief Executive Officer*
GILBERT M. GROSVENOR *Chairman of the Board*
NINA D. HOFFMAN *Senior Vice President*

Prepared by the Book Division
WILLIAM R. GRAY *Vice President and Director*
CHARLES KOGOD *Assistant Director*
BARBARA A. PAYNE *Editorial Director and Managing Editor*
DAVID GRIFFIN *Design Director*

Staff for this Book
KEVIN MULROY *Editor*
LISA LYTTON *Art Director*
CARL MEHLER *Director of Maps*
JOSEPH F. OCHLAK *Map Research*
MICHELLE H. PICARD *Map Production*
TIBOR G. TÓTH *Map Relief*
WILLIAM R. NEWCOTT *Legends Writer*
KEVIN CRAIG *Assistant Editor*
R. GARY COLBERT *Production Director*
KATHLEEN COLE *Production Assistant*
MEREDITH WILCOX *Illustrations Assistant*
PEGGY CANDORE *Assistant to the Director*
NATASHA KLAUSS *Staff Assistant*
KATHY BARBER *Indexer*

We gratefully acknowledge the assistance of contributing editors Barbara Payne and K. M. Kostyl.

Manufacturing and Quality Control
GEORGE V. WHITE *Director*
JOHN T. DUNN *Associate Director*
VINCENT P. RYAN *Manager*
JAMES J. SORENSEN *Budget Analyst*

The world's largest nonprofit scientific and educational organization, the National Geographic Society was founded in 1888 "for the increase and diffusion of geographic knowledge." Since then it has supported scientific exploration and spread information to its more than nine million members worldwide.

The National Geographic Society educates and inspires millions every day through magazines, books, television programs, videos, maps and atlases, research grants, the National Geography Bee, teacher workshops, and innovative classroom materials.

The Society is supported through membership dues and income from the sale of its educational products. Members receive NATIONAL GEOGRAPHIC magazine—the Society's official journal—discounts on Society products, and other benefits.

For more information about the National Geographic Society and its educational programs and publications, please call 1-800-NGS-LINE (647-5463), or write to the following address:

NATIONAL GEOGRAPHIC SOCIETY,
1145 17th Street N.W., Washington, D.C. 20036-4688 U.S.A.

Visit the Society's Web site at www.nationalgeographic.com.